access to h

Reforming Britain
181

access to history

Reforming Britain 1815–50

Michael Scott-Baumann

Hodder Murray
A MEMBER OF THE HODDER HEADLINE GROUP

The Publishers would like to thank the following for permission to reproduce copyright illustrations: © Bettmann/CORBIS, page 62; British Library, London, UK/Bridgeman Art Library, page 64; British Museum, London, UK/Bridgeman Art Library, page 24; Fotomas Index UK, page 121; © Hulton-Deutsch Collection/CORBIS, pages 99, 122; Mary Evans Picture Library, pages 15, 18, 22, 26, 63, 70, 117, 133, 137, 142; The National Archives, ref: HO44/27 pt.2 (1), page 96; © Michael Nicholson/CORBIS, pages 36, 138; Private Collection/ Bridgeman Art Library, page 120; Reproduced with permission of Punch, Ltd. www.punch.co.uk, page 140; Alison Scott-Baumann, page 21; Sheffield Galleries and Museum Trust, page 4; Courtesy of the Trustees of Sir John Soane's Museum, London/Bridgeman Art Library, page 56.

Every effort has been made to trace all copyright holders, but if any have been inadvertently overlooked the Publishers will be pleased to make the necessary arrangements at the first opportunity.

Although every effort has been made to ensure that website addresses are correct at time of going to press, Hodder Murray cannot be held responsible for the content of any website mentioned in this book. It is sometimes possible to find a relocated web page by typing in the address of the home page for a website in the URL window of your browser.

Orders: please contact Bookpoint Ltd, 130 Milton Park, Abingdon, Oxon OX14 4SB. Telephone: (44) 01235 827720. Fax: (44) 01235 400454. Lines are open 9.00–6.00, Monday to Saturday, with a 24-hour message answering service. Visit our website at www.hoddereducation.co.uk

First published in 2006 by
Hodder Murray, an imprint of Hodder Education,
a member of the Hodder Headline Group
338 Euston Road
London NW1 3BH

Impression number   10 9 8 7 6 5 4 3 2 1
Year   2010 2009 2008 2007 2006

Cover photo shows © Mary Evans Picture Library
Typeset in Baskerville 10/12pt and produced by Gray Publishing, Tunbridge Wells
Printed in Malta

A catalogue record for this title is available from the British Library

ISBN-10: 0 340 90707 X
ISBN-13: 978 0 340 90707 8

Contents

Dedication

Keith Randell (1943–2002)

The *Access to History* series was conceived and developed by Keith, who created a series to 'cater for students as they are, not as we might wish them to be'. He leaves a living legacy of a series that for over 20 years has provided a trusted, stimulating and well-loved accompaniment to post-16 study. Our aim with these new editions is to continue to offer students the best possible support for their studies.

1 Britain in 1815

POINTS TO CONSIDER

In 1815, Britain emerged from a long war with France. None of the fighting had taken place on British soil so life had seemed to carry on as usual for most British people. However, the country was experiencing huge economic and social changes and, in the years after 1815, these changes threatened to tear Britain apart. Trying to prevent this happening occupied the energies of nearly every government in the years from 1815 to 1850. Carrying out political, social and economic reforms was one way of keeping Britain intact and these reforms provide the main focus for this book. This first chapter sets the scene by examining:

- The main economic and social changes that were transforming Britain
- The political system

1 | Economy and Society

Key question
What was Britain like in 1815?

Today, we would hardly recognise the Britain of 1815. There were vast areas of forest and much of the rest of the landscape was farmland. Most people lived in villages, in the countryside, and worked in agriculture. Farming was by far the biggest employer. Most people never left the region in which they lived and most married someone from their own village or nearby. The country was sparsely populated: the total population of England, Wales and Scotland was 13 million (today it is about 55 million). The capital, London, had a population of a million but, when the first census was taken in 1801, no other city had a population of more than 100,000. The main means of transport, apart from walking, was on horseback. You could travel from one end of the country to the other, but it would take several days and several changes of horse.

Yet Britain in 1815 was changing, and it was changing more rapidly than any other country in Europe. The first thing that was changing was population. In the 10 years from 1810 to 1820,

This was the main form of travel, apart from walking, in 1815. It took several days to go from Edinburgh to London.

the population rose more quickly than at any other time in British history, before or since. But there were many other changes as well. Britain was in the throes of what later became known as the Industrial Revolution.

The Industrial Revolution

Britain was in the process of becoming the world's first industrial nation, although few people were aware of it at the time. Many of the changes were taking place quite gradually. Nevertheless, they were of fundamental importance because they were transforming the very way people lived and worked. Central to these revolutionary changes were new developments in technology. For instance, instead of relying almost solely on muscle power, more and more workshops, factories, mills and mines were using water, or even steam, to power the machines.

The textile industry

As an example, let us consider the textile industry. For a long time, Britain's main industry had been the production of cloth. Most of this was woollen but, as more and more cotton was imported from the USA, so woollen production was overtaken by the production of cotton cloth. In fact, by 1815, cotton cloth was Britain's largest export. All of this was made possible by changes in technology: a series of inventions in the eighteenth century

Key question
What were the main features of the Industrial Revolution?

had speeded up the processes of spinning and weaving. These inventions made use of new forms of power. First, the power of fast-flowing rivers could be harnessed to drive water wheels which, in turn, could drive spinning and weaving machines. Then, from the late eighteenth century, steam power began to be exploited. Factories burned coal to heat water to produce the steam that powered spinning and weaving machines.

There were still, it is true, far more **handloom weavers** producing woollen and cotton cloth in their homes and in small workshops than there were factory workers. However, the most advanced factories and mills were now being built on coalfields so that they had a ready supply of coal to power the new machines. Steam-driven machinery not only produced cloth, it could also be used to pump water from coalmines, thereby reducing the constant problem of flooding, and to provide the blast for iron-producing furnaces.

Key term

Handloom weaver
A person who used a hand-powered weaving machine.

Canals

Materials such as coal, iron and cotton were bulky and, particularly in the case of coal and iron, very heavy. Transporting them along Britain's roads, often bumpy or waterlogged, was slow and expensive. Here, the building of canals had made a big difference over the previous 50 years: Britain's rivers were now linked by canals. Over the next 50 years railways would further revolutionise both industry and communications.

The growth of factories and towns

The installation of large, heavy and expensive machinery led to the growth of factories employing not just 10 or 20, but hundreds of workers. Housing for these workers was built alongside the factories so that large new towns grew up. These were densely populated and polluted, with foul-smelling air and blackened buildings. In the 1830s, Sheffield was described as 'poisoned in its own excrement'.

The new factories and towns in the north of England, the Midlands, South Wales and the Scottish lowlands depended on a ready supply of cheap labour. This was made possible by the population rise that had been taking place since the mid-eighteenth century. Many of the factory workers were women and children. They were cheaper to employ and, for much of the work, they did not need special skills or training. In the cotton mills, 70 per cent of the work was carried out by women and children. Even down the mines, much of the unskilled work, such as filling and pushing coal carts, was done by children. With more work available and more opportunity to earn money in the towns and cities, women could afford to get married earlier. In 1821, nearly 50 per cent of the population was under 15 (today it is 20 per cent).

As the population rose and towns and cities grew, there were more mouths to feed. Fortunately, agriculture was able to respond. With improved drainage and **irrigation**, and new techniques of animal breeding and crop farming, agriculture was

Key term

Irrigation
The supply of water to agricultural land.

Sheffield in 1850. In 1801, the population of Sheffield was 46,000. By 1850, it was 135,000. What key features of the Industrial Revolution are shown in this picture?

able to meet the increased demand from the growing urban areas. Improvements in agriculture and transport enabled more and more urban workers to rely on a regular supply of cheap, plentiful food from the countryside.

Altogether, these changes in population and agriculture, the technological developments in the coal, iron and textile industries and improvements in transport constituted what historians have since come to call the Industrial Revolution.

A society under strain

It would be wrong to think that most people worked in factories. Factory production was concentrated in Lancashire, Yorkshire and the Scottish lowlands. This is where the great factory towns were: Manchester, Glasgow, Leeds and Bradford. But large factories were the exception in early nineteenth-century Britain. Even in the more advanced, mechanised cotton industry, more than half of those employed in the mills were working in factories with fewer than 100 employees. In fact, most of the industrial growth was due to the expansion of smaller workshops and factories. One historian has written:

> There were more cobblers and shoemakers, craftsmen working on their own or in small workshops, than there were male factory workers; and there were between three and four times as many working in the completely unmechanised building trades. Tailors outnumbered coalminers, and there were three blacksmiths for every man employed in making iron. (F.M.L. Thompson, *The Rise of Respectable Society*, Fontana, 1988.)

A great deal of industrial work was still carried out in the homes of hundreds of thousands of people in villages across Britain. The main differences between this domestic system of manufacture and the factory system are outlined in Table 1.1.

Key question
In what ways was Britain 'a society under strain'?

Table 1.1: The factory system and the domestic system in the textile industry

The domestic system	The factory system
Small-scale production	Large-scale production
Machines powered by muscle/humans	Machines powered by water or steam
Family unit as workforce	Large-scale workforce

Contemporary views on industrialisation

The new factories and the new cities attracted the attention of several writers in the nineteenth century. Some were very favourably impressed and optimistic:

Source A

It is to the **spinning jenny** and the steam engine that we must look as having been the true moving powers of our fleets and armies, and the chief support also of a long-continued agricultural prosperity. (George Porter, *Progress of the Nation*, 1847.)

1. In what ways could the spinning jenny and the steam engine have been 'the moving powers of our fleets and armies'?
2. How could they have been 'the chief support of a long-continued agricultural prosperity'?

Other commentators were more critical:

Source B

It is the Age of Machinery. Nothing is done directly or by hand; all is by rule and calculation. Our old ways of working are all discredited and thrown aside. On every hand, the living craftsman is driven from his workshop, to make room for a speedier, inanimate one. The shuttle drops from the fingers of the weaver, and falls into iron fingers that ply it faster. Men are grown mechanical in head and in heart, as well as in hand. They have lost faith in individual endeavour, and in natural force of any kind. Their whole efforts, attachments, opinions, turn on mechanism, and are of a mechanical character. (Adapted from Thomas Carlyle, *Signs of the Times*, 1829.)

3. Explain, in your own words, what Carlyle meant, referring to specific phrases in the source.

A modern historian has written:

Source C

A large proportion of the rural workers had long been used to manufacturing through their own part-time employment within the domestic system. Two things were different in factory labour. First, there was the relentless discipline of mechanisation. Here was the origin of the conveyor-belt mentality where man, the creator of the machine, was made its servant. The discipline of

Key term

Spinning jenny
A hand-driven machine which speeded up the process of spinning cotton into a thread that could then be used for weaving cloth.

the machine was reinforced by the authority of master or overlooker and the sombre instructions of the factory bell, summoning hands, not people. Second, the decision of whether and when to work was taken out of the hands of the individual and placed at the whim of impersonal market forces. An independent handworker worked when he pleased; a factory operative could only work when required to do so by the demands of the market. (Derek Fraser, *The Evolution of the British Welfare State*, 1973.)

4. List the points made by Fraser (Source C) that support the views expressed by Carlyle in Source B.
5. How do you explain the use of the phrase 'hands, not people' and 'operative'?
6. What is meant by 'the demands of the market' and why were these so different at this time to 50 years previously?

The threat to traditional craftsmen

Many skilled craftsmen felt threatened by the new methods of factory production. Handloom weavers, for instance, feared that they would lose out to the new machines, especially if there was a **depression** and the demand for cloth declined. Their skills, learned over a seven-year apprenticeship, no longer seemed so valuable. Besides, it was cheaper to employ women and children in the new factories. Not only did this threaten the men's livelihood: it appeared to threaten their family life as well. In the home, they worked together as a family unit. Now the factory foreman or supervisor might exercise more control over their families. And if they were forced to seek work in a factory, they would lose their independence: clocking in and clocking off for work, having to obey rules and regulations about when they could take a break.

Key question
Why did traditional craftsmen feel threatened?

Depression
A time when there is less demand for industrial or agricultural goods and so there are fewer jobs and more unemployment.

Key term

The pressure on food supply

An even greater cause of stress was pressure on food supply. We now know that agricultural production largely kept up with the rise in population but, to contemporaries, it was very worrying. When there were poor harvests, the situation was very precarious. There were widespread fears that population would outstrip food production and these fears were most vividly expressed by Thomas Malthus, a contemporary writer. One of his supporters wrote:

Key question
Why was there a fear of unrest, even of revolution?

Population must, if possible, be prevented from increasing beyond the means of subsistence [producing enough food to survive]. This can only be done by restraining people from marrying until they can bear the expenses of a family. Whatever other remedies may be prescribed, therefore, restrictions upon marriages of the poor are an indispensable part of the regime to be observed.

A modern historian has written:

> The fears of Mr. Malthus were not just fears of numbers of people, but fear of radical social change, even of revolution. ... Britain was unique in avoiding a violent revolution in the nineteenth century. But to early Victorians it seemed a matter of touch and go. (J.F.C. Harrison, *Early Victorian Britain, 1832–51*, Fontana, 1988.)

Urbanisation: the growth of cities and towns

One of the greatest worries was the rapid growth of new, industrial cities. This growth is shown in Figure 1.1 overleaf.

In 1851, just over a quarter of the adult inhabitants of Manchester, Glasgow and Bradford had been born in the town. Most had migrated from surrounding rural areas. This huge urban growth brought with it overcrowding, pollution and disease. It also increased the government's fear of revolution. Before we study the government's response to that threat, it is necessary to examine how Britain was governed at this time.

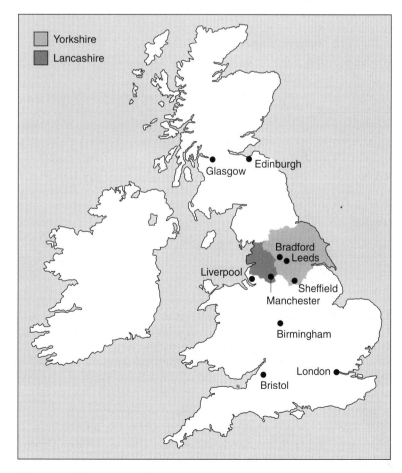

Map 1.1: The growth of industrial Britain. In 1801, London had a population of nearly a million. No other city had a population of more than 100,000. By 1851, 10 cities had populations of more than 100,000.

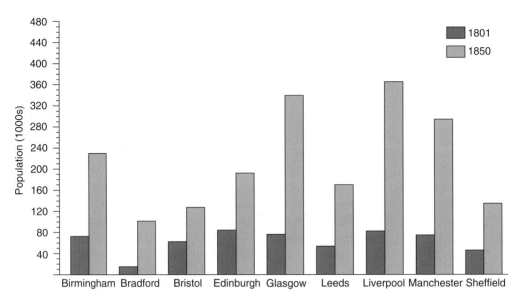

Figure 1.1: Population changes in British cities 1801–50. In these years, the population of London grew to over two million.

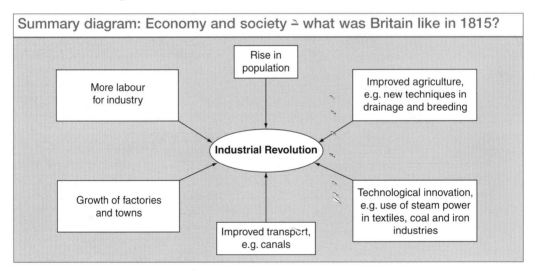

2 | The Political System

In 1815, as we have seen, Britain was undergoing sweeping economic and social changes. Yet the political system remained largely unchanged. At the very top of this system was the monarch. In 1815, George III was on the throne. He had been king since 1760, but he was ill; among his symptoms he had been found talking to trees at Windsor and, in 1811, he had been declared unfit to govern. His eldest son, George, became **Prince Regent** (and later king, in 1820, when his father died). The Prince Regent, for his part, was too lazy or incompetent to take much interest in government and politics so that the government of the country continued to be left more and more to the king's ministers.

Key question
What was the king's role?

Prince Regent
Title given to Prince George when he acted as monarch during his father's illness.

Key term

The king could still appoint and dismiss a Prime Minister and he could also insist on having a say in the appointment of other ministers. However, the monarch had to take account of the wishes of Parliament if he was to influence their policies and get them to agree to the taxes without which his government could not operate. Thus, if a parliamentary leader had a large body of support in the House of Commons, the king was usually obliged to make him Prime Minister. In 1815 that person was Lord Liverpool. Liverpool had already been Prime Minister for three years, and the Prince Regent relied very heavily on Liverpool and his Cabinet ministers to control Parliament and govern the land.

The landowning classes

Key question
In what ways did the landowning classes dominate British political life?

Both government and Parliament were dominated by the landowning classes. In fact, Britain was largely governed by a few thousand landowning families who, between them, owned more than half the agricultural land. Generation after generation inherited the land and, with it, the wide-ranging power and influence which they had wielded for hundreds of years. The most important of these landowning families were members of the **aristocracy**. Their ancestors had been made nobles (with titles like Lord, Duke, Viscount or Earl) by earlier kings and queens and so they had become members of the House of Lords.

Key term

Aristocracy
Nobles, or peers, who inherited titles giving them the right to sit in the House of Lords.

The landowning aristocracy assumed their right to supremacy to be natural. Their status was hereditary so that the right to a seat in the House of Lords was passed on to succeeding generations. The House of Lords was their central power base, but they had huge influence over the House of Commons as well. This was because nearly half of the Members of Parliament (MPs) owed their seats to peers (members of the House of Lords) and many were related to them. The landed classes held the highest positions in the Church, the armed services, the judiciary and the civil service. They also ruled the countryside and dominated local government.

The main responsibilities of the State, or central government, were limited to defence, the control of trade (through taxes and customs duties) and the supervision of law and order. (The government was not expected to provide schools and hospitals as it does today.) It was *local* government that most affected people in the nineteenth century.

The magistrates

Key question
Why were the magistrates so important in local government?

In the localities, as at the centre of government in London, it was the landowning classes who predominated. At the top of local society was the Lord-Lieutenant of the county who was usually the largest landowner. He was the king's representative in the county and reported back to the central government in London. Under him were the magistrates or Justices of the Peace (JPs). These were the men who bore the main burden of governing Britain.

The magistrates had the major responsibility for preserving peace and for preventing crime and disorder in an age when there was no professional police force. They were mostly landowners, while about a quarter were ministers of the Church of England. Magistrates were unpaid and untrained. As men of property (they were often the biggest employers in a locality) or as Church ministers, they possessed considerable status while their role as magistrates brought them added power and influence. They had the authority to arrest, fine and imprison people for minor offences and to recommend trial by a higher court for major offences. They also saw to the upkeep of roads and bridges and were responsible for prisons and the care of the poor.

Many people were dependent on the landowning magistrates, as their tenants or hired labourers, so great respect was paid to them. If, however, the magistrates proved unable to deal with local disorder, they could call out the yeomanry, a mounted volunteer force which, like the magistrates, was unpaid and consisted largely of men of property. In the case of a major disturbance, and there were many in the years after 1815, the central government could be asked to send in troops to restore order.

The Houses of Parliament

Parliament consisted of two houses, as it does today. The House of Lords was made up of hereditary peers whereas the Commons was elected. However, only a small percentage of the male population had the right to vote. This is explained more fully in Chapter 4.

The majority of MPs were landowners, although an increasing number were men who had made their money in trade or industry. Most MPs belonged to either the Tory or the Whig party. The main similarities and differences between these two parties are summarised in the table opposite.

A threat of revolution?

In 1815, the population was rising rapidly. If there was a poor harvest, as there was in 1816, and bread prices rose, millions faced the prospect of great hunger, if not starvation. 'Distress', as contemporaries called it, undoubtedly contributed to the growth of working-class unrest in the period after 1815. The government reacted to such unrest and, in particular, to demands from the working classes for a voice in Parliament, with great alarm and fear. They remembered from their youth hearing about the overthrow of the monarchy and the ruling classes in the **French Revolution**. This period of popular agitation, and the government's response to it, is the subject of the Chapter 2.

> **Key question**
> How clear were the distinctions between Tories and Whigs?

> **Key term**
> **French Revolution**
> A series of events, starting in 1789, which led to the fall of the monarchy and of the aristocracy in France.

Tories and Whigs
These parties were loose groupings that had originally developed out of the struggle between king and Parliament in the Civil War of the seventeenth century. They were not as well organised as modern political parties.

Both were dominated by landowning families and family networks often determined whether you became Tory or Whig.

Both parties were led by Anglicans, i.e. members of the Church of England, which was the official State church.

There were more similarities, in background and belief, than there were differences between the two parties in 1815.

The Tories	*The Whigs*
The Tories were particularly keen to defend the power of the monarch and the Church of England.	The Whigs were more likely to question the power of the monarch and to defend the power of Parliament.
Nearly all the Tories came from landowning backgrounds.	Although their leaders were mostly landowners, an increasing number of Whig MPs came from industrial or commercial backgrounds.
The Tories were more protective of the privileges of the Church of England.	Whigs were more sympathetic to, and had more support from, **Nonconformists**.
The Tories were more resistant to change and more fearful of the ideas of the French Revolution.	The Whigs began to demand reform of Parliament in the late 1820s.

Key term

Nonconformists
Baptists, Quakers, Presbyterians and Methodists, etc.: Protestants, but not members of the Church of England.

Summary diagram: The political system

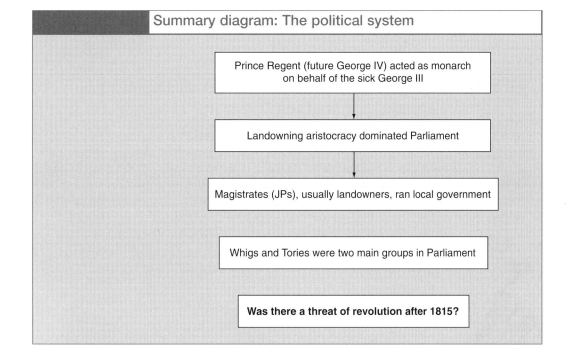

Prince Regent (future George IV) acted as monarch on behalf of the sick George III

Landowning aristocracy dominated Parliament

Magistrates (JPs), usually landowners, ran local government

Whigs and Tories were two main groups in Parliament

Was there a threat of revolution after 1815?

Study Guide

Read Section 1, 'Economy and Society' (pages 1–8) again and answer the following questions:

(a) What social problems might the huge increase in population have led to?
(b) How might these problems contribute to the fear of revolution?
(c) From what you have learned in this chapter, make a list of the stresses and strains that characterised Britain in 1815. Put them in order of importance and discuss them in class.

POINTS TO CONSIDER
At the end of the war against France, most people
expected peace and prosperity; instead, there followed five
years of hunger, unemployment and a wave of popular
protest. This chapter will examine:

- The effects of the war with France
- The radical campaign in the country 1815–20
- The government response to popular protest

Key dates

1810–11		Luddite risings
1815		End of war with France
		Corn Laws
1816–17		Harsh winter; national petitioning campaign
1816	December	Spa Fields meeting; suspension of Habeas Corpus
1817	March	March of the Blanketeers
		Government ban on large meetings
	June	Pentrich Rising
1819	August	'Peterloo massacre'
		The Six Acts
1820		Cato Street Conspiracy
1820s		Trade improved and popular protest subsided

1 | The Effects of the War with France

Key question
What pressure for
reform was there
before 1815?

In the early 1790s, before the war with France (1793–1815), there
had been some pressure for reform of Parliament. The reformers
criticised what they saw as a corrupt and inefficient government.
They believed that Parliament was completely dominated by the
king and his ministers, and that it was very difficult for men with
independent views to get a hearing. In the early days of the
French Revolution, which started in 1789, the news from France
had encouraged British reformers to call for changes in the way
Britain was governed.

Some of the reformers had come from the richer, propertied classes. But there was also support for **parliamentary reform** from the poorer sections of society. Many of the working classes were inspired by the writings of Tom Paine. Even if they could not read his work, they heard passages read out in pubs and clubs and in their homes. Paine's book, the *Rights of Man*, advocated sweeping reforms to improve the lives of working men and women. For instance, he called for free education for all and pensions for the elderly. Above all, he called for **universal manhood suffrage** so that all men, not just the rich or property owners, had the right to vote for their Member of Parliament. Only then, he said, would ordinary working men get elected and have the opportunity to pass laws through Parliament that would benefit them.

This reform campaign did not last long. The majority of the upper classes were opposed to the demands for change. They were even more horrified when they heard that the revolution in France had turned to violence and killings and that French revolutionary forces had invaded Belgium and the Netherlands. After Britain went to war in 1793, the government persuaded Parliament to pass tough laws to suppress the agitation for reform in Britain. In fact, the majority of British people, rich or poor, were intensely loyal. Thousands volunteered to fight in the army and in the civil defence forces that would defend Britain if invaded. In this atmosphere of repression and patriotism, the reform movement quietened down.

Luddism

The campaign for reform never died out completely. In the 1800s, when the threat of invasion receded, it slowly began to be revived. But something quite new also emerged in 1810–11. There were reports of men with blackened faces attacking factories and mills by night. These reports came from the industrial towns and villages of Nottinghamshire, Lancashire and Yorkshire. Most of the attacks were on mills and factories that had installed new machines, especially in the textile industry, and it was often these new machines that were singled out for destruction. The houses of the owners were also targeted, although attacks on people were rare. The perpetrators were mostly skilled men who still used traditional, hand-operated machinery for spinning, weaving and other processes. These craftsmen felt their jobs and livelihoods to be under threat now that the population was rising and more and more women and children were being employed to mind the machines in the new mills and factories.

The attackers were known as Luddites after a person called Ned Ludd who was said to inspire and lead these men. He was portrayed as a kind of Robin Hood figure, but it is unlikely that he ever existed. There is little written evidence of Luddism, except from the reports of factory owners, magistrates and the government. It is likely that most of those directly involved in the night-time raids were illiterate: certainly the notes left, often threatening attack if the machines were not removed, suggest that. One such note is shown on page 16.

Key terms

Parliamentary reform
Only a small number of people were allowed to vote for MPs. Parliamentary reform primarily meant granting this right to more people.

Universal manhood suffrage
The right to vote for all men.

Key question
Who were the Luddites?

The mythical Ned Ludd leading his followers into the attack. Some Luddites are known to have disguised themselves as women, hence he is shown wearing a dress.

Key term

Capital offence
A crime carrying the death penalty.

However, the poor handwriting might have been a deliberate ploy to maintain the secrecy of the author's identity. The bands of men were keen to keep their activities secret to escape detection. Thousands of troops were stationed in the North and Midlands to counter the Luddite threat. Machine breaking was made a **capital offence**. After several executions and the return of better economic conditions, Luddite outbreaks petered out. But they had shocked the authorities.

The attacks were not politically motivated; they were not part of an organised campaign for political rights. Most of these incidents were locally organised and there is little evidence of co-ordinated planning across the counties affected. However, when the war ended, things were to change and a widespread, national agitation for parliamentary reform emerged.

We hear in formed that you got Shear in mee sheens and if you Dont Pull them Down in A Forght Nights time wee will pull them Down for you wee will you Damd infernold Dog. And Bee four Almighty God we will burn down all the Mills that heave Heavy Shearing me Shens in we will cut out Hall your Damd Hearts as do keep them and we will meock the rest Heat them or else We will seave them the seam.

King Ned Ludd.

Luddite handwriting.

The end of the war 1815

When the 20-year war with France finally ended in 1815, all Britons hoped for a return to peace and prosperity. Yet the next five years were to be marked by unemployment, hunger, discontent and violence. Above all, they were to be years of widespread agitation for reform of Parliament.

Many of those campaigning for reform were referred to as **radicals**, meaning that they wanted major, fundamental reform, not just tinkering with the system. The radicals had a small number of supporters in the House of Commons. In the later stages of the war against France, they had looked to these MPs as leaders, hoping that they could persuade Parliament to listen to their grievances and consider their demands. But most of these parliamentary reformers did not go as far as to advocate complete manhood suffrage. Instead, MPs like Sir Francis Burdett called for the vote for all householders (people who owned or rented a house of their own) or for all who paid taxes directly to the government. However, what developed after 1815 was a widespread campaign for complete manhood suffrage so as to secure the vote for all adult men. Moreover, the most prominent leaders of this agitation were more concerned with building up a mass movement across the country than with cultivating the support of individual MPs. Before we examine this new, radical campaign, we need to look more closely at the economic and political situation in Britain at the end of the war in 1815.

Britain emerged from the war victorious, and as the wealthiest and most powerful nation on earth. Yet the conflict had been very expensive. To finance the war, the government had had to increase taxes. It had also borrowed a vast amount of money. Most of these loans had come from a fairly small number of wealthy people. These '**fundholders**' would not only have to be

Key question
What were the effects of the end of the war?

Key date

End of the war with France: 1815

Key terms

Radicals
Those who believed in the need for radical, or fundamental, reform.

Fundholders
Those who had lent the government money during the French wars.

paid back one day; they would also have to be paid annual interest on the loans. This meant that the government would have to raise money in tax to pay the interest, let alone to pay off the debt completely. In the years after the war, interest paid on these loans used up 80 per cent of government income.

During the war, the government had introduced a new tax, an income tax, which only the rich, for obvious reasons, paid. When the war ended, the MPs reminded the government of their promise that income tax would only be temporary, a war-time measure. Most MPs now insisted that income tax be dropped and the government was forced to give way. Instead of this **direct tax**, Parliament now introduced new **indirect taxes**. These included taxes on everyday items such as sugar, tea, soap, candles, beer and tobacco. They were collected indirectly, through the increased costs of these items. These taxes would hit the poor just as hard as the rich. In fact, they would hit the poor much harder since a much higher percentage of their income would be spent on these items.

On top of increased taxation came unemployment. Over 300,000 men returned from war service looking for work and, in those days, there were no pensions or allowances paid to war veterans as we might expect today. Furthermore, industries such as textiles (producing army uniforms) and coal, iron and engineering (producing weapons) now found that government contracts dried up and so more workers were laid off. Even worse was to follow when the government decided to ban imports of foreign wheat.

The Corn Laws 1815

During the war Britain had had to rely almost exclusively on its own farmers to produce the wheat needed to make bread. This was especially so during the many years when the French blockaded western Europe and tried to stop all trade between Britain and the continent. Now that the war had ended, landowners, who dominated Parliament, demanded a ban on imports of foreign wheat. They said that Britain needed to be self-sufficient in case of another war and because the population was rising so quickly. They knew that hunger and famine had been one of the major causes of the French Revolution and were determined to avoid such a revolution in Britain. They also reminded Parliament that agriculture employed many more people than any other industry and claimed that hundreds of thousands of farmers (and farm labourers) could be thrown out of work if Britain was flooded with cheap foreign wheat.

However, critics of the government saw it very differently. When the **Corn Laws** were passed in 1815, the government's opponents said it was purely '**class legislation**', passed by a landowning Parliament for completely selfish reasons. They accused Parliament of passing the laws simply to safeguard landowners' profits and rents. It was taxes like these that convinced many outside Parliament that they could never expect fairness and justice unless the system of elections to Parliament was completely changed. In other words, they would have to resort to political means in order to improve their living conditions.

Key terms

Direct taxes
Taxes paid directly to the State, such as income tax.

Indirect taxes
Taxes paid as part of the price on purchases.

Key question
What were the Corn Laws?

Key terms

Corn Laws
Tariffs, or import duties, on foreign wheat. Importing wheat was banned until British wheat reached 80 shillings (£4) a quarter (about 13 kg).

Class legislation
A law passed to favour a particular class, in this case the landed class.

'The Blessings of Peace or the Curse of the Corn Bill', a cartoon by George Cruikshank, 1815. What are the views, as shown in the cartoon, of (a) the French traders, (b) the English landlords and (c) the English worker?

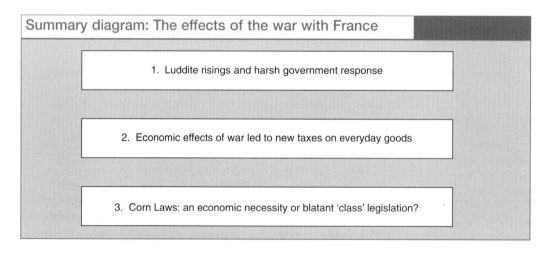

Summary diagram: The effects of the war with France

1. Luddite risings and harsh government response

2. Economic effects of war led to new taxes on everyday goods

3. Corn Laws: an economic necessity or blatant 'class' legislation?

2 | The Radical Campaign in the Country 1815–20

During the years 1815–20, radical agitation outside Parliament took three main forms. These were:

- the campaign in the press
- political clubs
- public meetings.

Key question
Why did so many working people demand parliamentary reform?

The campaign in the press

The first was the campaign in the press. The 'father' of all newspaper agitators was Major John Cartwright. A gentleman-farmer by background, he had been in the forefront of radical politics for 40 years. In the later years of the Napoleonic Wars he had spent months travelling in the Midlands, the North and Scotland to see for himself how these areas had been affected by economic hardship. He had worked hard to convert his listeners and readers to the cause of parliamentary reform and to establish links between reformers across the country.

But the most widely read of all journalists was **William Cobbett**. Like Cartwright, he had also travelled thousands of miles round Britain, by horseback, in order to win support and learn more about living and working conditions. He published a *Weekly Political Register*. When it was published as a short pamphlet for two pence a week, it was read by thousands. And for every person who read it, there were many more who found out from friends, family or workmates what it said.

Cobbett had no doubt who was responsible for the people's suffering. He attacked the government and their hangers-on. In particular, he singled out the 'placemen' who received incomes, paid for from taxation, for the 'places' they held in government. He also attacked the government 'pensioners' who received money when they retired. He railed against the 'fundholders', those who had lent money to the government and lived off the income they received in interest. He said they were 'parasites' and 'taxeaters'. He accused the governing classes of being 'unproductive' and 'idle' and contrasted them with the 'industrious classes', the working men and women who starved so that the rich could live in luxury. He championed the cause of working people and he knew exactly where to lay the blame for the workers' suffering, as he wrote in November 1816 in the *Political Register*:

Key question
What type of tax is Cobbett condemning?

> As to the causes of our present miseries, it is the enormous amount of taxes, which the government compels us to pay for the support of its army, its placemen, its pensioners etc. and for the payment of the interest of its debt. That this is the real cause has been a thousand times proved; and it is now so acknowledged by the creatures of the government themselves. The tax gatherers do not, indeed, come to you and demand money of you: but, there are few articles which you use, in the purchase of which you do not pay a tax.

The winter of 1816–17 was very harsh. There had been a poor harvest in the summer and bread prices rose higher than they had ever been before. Cobbett's arguments found an enthusiastic response among the working classes. It was said that Cobbett's writings were being read in nearly every cottage in south Lancashire and the east Midlands in the winter of 1816–17. Samuel Bamford, a Lancashire radical and weaver, wrote this about him in his book *Passages in the Life of a Radical* in 1839:

Key term
William Cobbett
His *Political Register* was the most widely read radical journal in the years after 1815. To avoid arrest, he fled to the USA in 1817, returning in 1819. In 1832, he became the radical MP for Oldham, Lancashire.

[Cobbett's] influence was speedily visible; he directed his readers to the true cause of their sufferings – misgovernment; and to its proper corrective – parliamentary reform.

Political clubs

Many of Cobbett's readers attended meetings in pubs, chapels and cottages in these years, and the radical club, where these people gathered, was the second form of agitation. The best known of these was the Hampden Club founded in 1812. It was named after John Hampden, a harsh critic of the king's government at the start of the civil war in the seventeenth century. This club had been established by Cartwright and others to win over 'respectable' support for reform. Most 'respectable' people were far too afraid of radical ideas, fearing it might lead to revolution, and not many joined. However, working men set up Hampden Clubs in the industrial areas of Lancashire, Yorkshire and the Midlands. They were open to any man able to pay a penny a week subscription. This money could then be used to finance the publication of pamphlets supporting manhood suffrage and the abolition of the Corn Laws.

In 1816–17, the Hampden Clubs organised a petitioning campaign. The presentation of a petition to Parliament was a long-established and legal method of expressing public opinion. In hundreds of villages and towns, especially in industrial areas, meetings were held and signatures collected. All demanded reform of Parliament and most called for an end to the Corn Laws and for fairer taxes. Some of the strongest support was in Lancashire where thousands of handloom weavers, threatened with the loss of their jobs, were at the forefront of the agitation. Villages and towns across the country held meetings and selected representatives to attend a national meeting in London.

Public meetings

The third form of radical agitation was the public meeting. This is most closely associated with the name of Henry Hunt. Like Cartwright and Cobbett, he came from a farming background. Known as Orator Hunt because of his fiery speeches, he became a hero to the working classes. He had no interest in winning the support of 'gentleman reformers'. Instead, he looked to huge outdoor meetings, attended by 'members unlimited', to rouse the masses and provide a springboard for a rising. He didn't want any riots: he believed that it was by being well organised, orderly and peaceful that the masses could demonstrate their newfound power and discipline. In the face of meetings of such huge numbers, the government would find it hard to resist the people's demands. This method was known as the 'mass platform': massive demonstrations, and the collection of thousands of signatures, for petitions to Parliament, would form the platform for putting irresistible pressure on Parliament to reform itself. The largest meetings were held in cities such as Manchester, Birmingham and London.

Key question
What was achieved by the Hampden Clubs?

Spa Fields meeting, London, December 1816

In December 1816 a huge meeting was held at Spa Fields in London. Henry Hunt was due to address the crowd. The atmosphere was like that of a carnival. People in their thousands poured into the city: whole families, clubs and communities, both from within the city and from outlying villages. There were banners and bands, market stalls and slogans. Before the meeting, leaflets were circulated among the crowd. One of these called for:

BRITONS TO ARMS!

THE WHOLE COUNTRY WAITS THE SIGNAL FROM LONDON TO FLY TO ARMS! HASTE, BREAK OPEN GUNSMITHS AND OTHER LIKELY PLACES to find arms! Run all constables who touch a man of us; no rise of bread; no Regent; no Castlereagh, off with their heads; no placemen, no taxes, no bishops.

Before Hunt arrived a small section of the crowd rioted, breaking into gunshops, seizing weapons and marching towards the Tower of London. The riots lasted for several hours and there was looting. But the majority of the crowd were peaceful. They were also loyal and, when the band played the national anthem, thousands joined in the singing of 'God Save the King'. When Hunt arrived, they heard him call for lower taxes and the reform of Parliament.

In 1817, Parliament received over 700 petitions. Some had hundreds of signatures, others had thousands. Although there were a few radical MPs and some members of the Whig party were sympathetic, most members of Parliament were afraid of this demonstration of popular feeling. They certainly did not want to grant the vote to all men. The petitions were ignored or dismissed.

Placards at the Spa Fields meeting, December 1816.

3 | The Government Response to Popular Protest

The government knew that hunger and hardship motivated many of the demonstrators. The Home Secretary, Lord Sidmouth, had written to his brother in the summer of 1816: 'It is to the autumn and winter that I look with anxiety'. He knew that was when the effects of a bad harvest and a depression in trade would hit hardest. The government also felt threatened. These demonstrations smacked of revolution, especially when they turned violent. When the Regent's coach was attacked soon after the Spa Fields riots, the government suspended the law of **Habeas Corpus**. This meant that people could now be arrested and held without trial: they would not have to be charged with a specific offence or appear before a court. They could be arrested and imprisoned simply on suspicion of being a revolutionary.

Habeas Corpus The law that anyone arrested had to be charged with an offence and brought before a court. After the Latin for 'you have the body'.

Key term

Profile: Henry Hunt 1773–1835

1773 – Born
1810 – Imprisoned for assault
1816 – Spoke at Spa Fields meeting in London
1819 – Main speaker at St Peter's Fields meeting in Manchester
  – Arrested, tried and imprisoned
1821 – Released from prison
1830 – Became MP for Preston
1833 – Lost his seat in Parliament and retired from politics
1835 – Died

Henry Hunt came from a prosperous Wiltshire farming family. As a young man he became involved in radical politics and, while in prison, he met William Cobbett. On his release, he campaigned for universal manhood suffrage and, in the years after 1815, he became the most prominent, and the most popular, radical leader. A folk hero, he was distinguished by his white top hat and his flamboyant personality. He was well known for his rousing speeches and thousands would walk for miles to hear him speak at big open-air meetings. He was the main speaker at the Peterloo meeting in Manchester in 1819; he was arrested and later imprisoned for two years for his part in the episode.

  He became MP for Preston in 1830. This was a 'popular' constituency, with a large electorate even before the Reform Act and, in the 1830 election, Hunt defeated the anti-reform, Tory candidate. Hunt opposed the 1832 Reform Act (see page 64) because it did not grant the vote to working men.

Key question
What was the government's response to popular protest?

Key date
Suspension of Habeas Corpus: 1817

The March of the Blanketeers, March 1817

On 10 March 1817, a crowd gathered in Manchester. They planned to organise a protest march to London where a petition would be handed to the Regent. This demanded parliamentary reform, the abolition of the Corn Laws and the re-introduction of Habeas Corpus. It also listed economic grievances concerning unemployment and high taxes. In the event, about 300 marchers set off. Many were unemployed handloom weavers. They were hopeful that they would win support and attract more marchers on the way. They expected to be put up at night by friendly locals but each carried a blanket in case they had to sleep out. They did not get very far. They were stopped by troops in Stockport, only a few miles from Manchester. There was some fighting, one man was shot and several were wounded.

In the same month, Parliament passed an Act that made it illegal to hold a meeting of more than 50 people. With large meetings banned and Habeas Corpus suspended, the radicals were forced underground and into secrecy. The planning of large meetings and the co-ordination of their activities now became far more difficult. False names and secret codes were adopted. The government resorted to the use of spies and informers. These men would pretend to be agitators, infiltrate radical groups and encourage uprisings. They would help in the planning of such risings and then let the government know the details. In this way, the authorities would be ready to catch the rebels red-handed.

The Pentrich Rising, June 1817

The most famous government spy was known simply as 'Oliver'. He infiltrated a group of discontented workers in Derbyshire and led them to believe that, if they rose up and marched on Nottingham, their rising would be the start of a national rebellion and they would receive support from many other parts of the country. On a rainy night in June 1817, about 200 men with pikes, forks and a few guns set off from Pentrich in Derbyshire to march to Nottingham. When they arrived in Nottingham, they were met by troops and rounded up. Following a trial, the leaders were hanged and 30 were transported. The trial and executions may have served as a deterrent to other agitators, but the government's involvement led to a public outcry. The last words uttered by one of the rebels on the scaffold were: 'This is the work of the government and Oliver'.

Peterloo, August 1819

Key question
What were the results of the 'Peterloo massacre'?

In 1818, there was a slight improvement in trade and a fall in unemployment. For a short time, there was some relief from the hardship of the previous two years. The law on Habeas Corpus was no longer suspended and the ban on large meetings was now lifted. In 1819, four huge meetings were planned as a demonstration of radical, working-class strength. The last one was to take place in St Peter's Fields, Manchester, in August.

Radical clubs and political unions in industrial Lancashire prepared for the big day. Some took part in military-style drilling

'Manchester heroes', a cartoon by George Cruikshank. What is the message of this cartoon? How effective do you think such images were in the politics of the time?

before marching into Manchester. Whole families turned out in their 'Sunday best', keen to take the opportunity to hear Orator Hunt, 'the intrepid champion of the people's rights', as he was known in the north. There were brass bands and, when the marchers heard the national anthem played, 'the people for the most part took off their hats', according to one eyewitness. Ex-soldiers helped to marshal the crowds and keep order. There were probably over 60,000 present.

Faced by this show of strength, the Manchester magistrates decided to 'bring the matter to issue'. One of them declared: 'If the agitators of the country determine to persevere in their meeting, it will necessarily prove a trial of strength and there must be a conflict.'

The local authorities prepared themselves. The yeomanry, a volunteer cavalry force mostly made up of Manchester businessmen, traders and shopkeepers, were called up and professional troops were on stand-by. The magistrates gave the order for the arrest of Henry Hunt. As the yeomanry tried to reach him the crowd closed ranks to stop them doing so. In the panic that followed, some of the yeomanry used their swords to clear a path and later the troops were sent in.

There are many conflicting opinions about what exactly happened. Some said the yeomanry were drunk. They were certainly inexperienced, probably afraid for their lives. What we do know is that 11 people were killed and 400 injured, many of them crushed in the stampede as they tried to escape. Among the dead were two women and a child. The event became known as 'Peterloo', a mocking comparison with the British victory at the Battle of Waterloo in 1815.

There was an outcry in the press, including *The Times* and other middle-class papers. The government came in for criticism when they congratulated the Manchester magistrates for their 'prompt, decisive and efficient measures for the preservation of public tranquillity'. As the story of what happened was told and retold, the radicals attracted more and more sympathy and support while the government became increasingly unpopular.

The Six Acts 1819
Yet it was the government that now took the initiative and went on the offensive; they rushed the Six Acts through Parliament. These laws were soon dubbed the 'Gagging Acts' by their opponents. The Acts:

- banned military-style drilling and training
- gave magistrates increased powers to search for arms
- banned public meetings of over 50 people unless they had magistrates' permission
- speeded up trials
- imposed further restrictions on the press
- increased the tax, or Stamp Duty, on newspapers so as to make radical writings, like those of Cobbett, too expensive for poorer people.

These tough laws enabled the authorities to suppress political activity further. Then, in March 1820, the leaders of the St Peter's Fields meeting, including Henry Hunt, were put on trial and imprisoned for 'assembling with unlawful banners at an unlawful meeting for the purpose of exciting discontent'. Hunt was released in October 1822.

The Cato Street Conspiracy 1820
There was one, final, dramatic event in this period of radical agitation. In 1820, a group of extremists plotted to kill the members of the Cabinet in the so-called Cato Street Conspiracy. The group was infiltrated and arrested. Very few of the reformers at that time would have supported such revolutionary violence and, not surprisingly, there was little complaint when the plotters were executed.

The decline of popular protest
In the early 1820s trade improved. With the arrest of their leaders and an economic recovery underway, popular support for radical politics subsided. The post-war movement had built up a solid body of working-class support but the government and most of the property-owning classes were determined not to give way to demands for manhood suffrage. The government kept its nerve, and it had a strong and loyal army to rely on. The lack of middle-class support for reform made it easier for the government to

Key date

Trade improved and popular protest subsided: 1820s

'Free Born Englishman!', a Cruikshank cartoon commenting on the Six Acts in 1819. In how many ways was this Englishman gagged? How closely does the cartoon reflect the terms of the Six Acts?

The Queen Caroline affair 1820–1

There was one episode that had little to do with the campaign for parliamentary reform but which caused further trouble for the government. In 1820, King George III died and his son George, the Prince Regent, became king. The new king, George IV, had been married to a German princess, Caroline of Brunswick, in 1795 but they had separated several years before he was enthroned. Caroline lived on the continent and, like her husband, she had had many affairs. When George became king in 1820, she decided to return to England and assert her right to be queen. She even published a letter in the press in which she said that 'England is my real home to which I shall immediately fly'.

George, however, had very different ideas. The new king looked to the government, the king's government, to deal with her. She was offered a large sum of money to stay away, but she refused. The king then ordered the government to introduce a bill in Parliament that would end the marriage and prevent her becoming queen. She appealed to the press, who were happy to take up her cause against an unpopular new monarch who was seen as bad-tempered and loose-living. The Whigs also took up her cause, partly in order to embarrass the Tory government. Meetings in support of Caroline, who was portrayed as the innocent victim, were held across the country. The government was forced to drop its bill and eventually Caroline accepted a large pension. But that did not stop her trying to gatecrash the coronation at Westminster Abbey in July 1821. A month later, she caught a fever and died.

contain the campaign. The radicals had learned their lesson the hard way and, when the reform movement revived in 1830, they strove to maintain a good working alliance with the middle-class supporters of parliamentary reform.

How harsh was the government in its response to the radical threat?

The Tory government has often been portrayed as unnecessarily harsh in dealing with popular agitation. However, in making our judgements we must remember the circumstances of the time. For instance, governments were not expected then to provide relief from poverty. That was the responsibility of the local authorities. The government's priority was to defend the country from both external and internal threat. On the next page is a summary of arguments on both sides.

How harsh was the government in its response to popular protest?

The government was harsh	The government was moderate
The Corn Laws forced up bread prices.	Most of the discontent was not the fault of the government.
New taxes on common articles of consumption hit the poor hardest.	Population increase forced up bread prices.
Suspension of Habeas Corpus in 1817 was an unnecessary breach of civil rights.	Industrial changes (e.g. use of steam power) were bound to threaten jobs of traditional craftsmen.
The use of spies and informers was excessive. They had an incentive to exaggerate: they would receive higher pay.	End of war meant further loss of jobs.
	Long war made high taxes and the need to repay loans unavoidable.
The arrest of the Blanketeers was unlawful and unnecessary.	Corn Laws protected agriculture, Britain's biggest employer.
The government supported the magistrates who were responsible for the 'Peterloo massacre'.	The government did not have a modern police force so had to make use of spies and informers.
Most of the demonstrations were peaceful, attended by women and children.	Government had to rely on local authorities to keep order and prevent unrest in the regions. They had to support them even when they made mistakes, as at Peterloo.
Only a tiny minority of people supported revolutionary violence. The government had exaggerated fears of revolution, a hangover from the days of the French Revolution.	There were a number of dangerous revolutionaries, as seen in the Pentrich Rising and Cato Street Conspiracy.
	The suspension of Habeas Corpus was only temporary. All those arrested after the Spa Fields riot were released within a year.
	Some of the Six Acts were quite reasonable, e.g. the ban on military training.

Summary diagram: The radical campaign and government response 1815–20

Radical agitation: • radical press   • political clubs   • mass meetings

Radical threat	and	**Government response**
Spa Fields	⟶	Suspension of Habeas Corpus
March of Blanketeers	⟶	Ban on public meetings
Pentrich Rising	⟶	Use of spies and informers
Peterloo	⟶	Six Acts

Study Guide: AS Questions

In the style of AQA

Study the following sources and answer the questions that follow:

Source A

Adapted from: The Making of the English Working Class, *1963, by E.P. Thompson.*

The autumn of 1816 was a period of extreme misery and post-war unemployment, affecting equally Lancashire, Yorkshire, the Birmingham trades and London. At the same time, London was full of discharged soldiers and sailors.

Source B

Adapted from a speech made by Henry Hunt in 1816.

I condemn the petty shopkeepers and little tradesmen who set themselves up as a sort of privileged class, above the factory worker, the craftsman, the mechanic and the labourer.

Source C

From: Luddism to the First Reform Bill, *1986, by J.R. Dinwiddy.*

The radicals tried to ensure that their meetings were orderly and could not be branded as breaches of the peace; at the same time they tried to mobilise people in such numbers and to arouse such enthusiasm for the cause that parliament and the ruling classes would be made to feel that resistance was hopeless.

(a) **Use Source A and your own knowledge**
Explain briefly what is meant by 'extreme misery and post-war unemployment' in the context of the period 1815–20. (3 marks)

(b) **Use Source B and your own knowledge**
Explain how useful this source is as evidence of the type of people who supported radical reform in this period. (7 marks)

(c) **Use Sources A, B and C and your own knowledge**
'The failure of the popular movement to achieve parliamentary reform in the period 1815 to 1820 was primarily the result of the actions of a harsh, repressive government.' Explain why you agree or disagree with this statement. (15 marks)

Exam tips

The cross-references are intended to take you straight to the material that will help you to answer the questions.

(a) In question **(a)** you should show that 'post-war unemployment' refers to the unemployment following the end of the war in 1815 and is partly explained by 'discharged soldiers and sailors'. To explain 'extreme misery', you might also refer to:

- effects of poor harvests, Corn Laws and increased taxation on the poor

- loss of government contracts after end of war, creating 'unemployment' and 'misery' in textile and iron industries (pages 16–17).

(b) You have to evaluate the usefulness of the source in question **(b)**, in order to:

- show that you understand who Henry Hunt was, his views on parliamentary reform and how it might be achieved
- indicate any considerations that might limit the usefulness of the source, e.g. nature of his audience, whether Hunt was typical of radical leaders in seeing shopkeepers and tradesmen as a threat
- judge whether you think men like Hunt shaped, or responded to, those sections of society that supported radical reform (pages 18–25).

(c) Question **(c)** carries most of the marks, so you need to write a mini-essay. You need to focus on the main issue raised by the question (i.e. a harsh and repressive government being the main reason for failure of the popular movement) and this should then be balanced against other factors leading to a judgement which shows whether you agree or disagree. There is not much support for the statement in the sources. However, using knowledge gained from this chapter, you might explain:

- the use of spies and informers to uncover plots and catch ringleaders
- a government and Parliament determined to resist demands as extreme as those for complete manhood suffrage
- a loyal army and the courts ready to back up the government.

All of these could show a strong and determined government but were these also the signs of a harsh, repressive government? You should use the sources, as instructed in the question, and they might suggest other reasons for the failure to achieve parliamentary reform, for example:

- Source A. Were the reformers motivated more by economic factors ('extreme misery and post-war unemployment') than by political aspirations? Was it 'hunger politics' that motivated the masses so that the government only had to weather mass support in times of economic hardship?
- Source B. Did leaders like Henry Hunt alienate middle-class support and thus lose the added numbers, influence, money and connections that would have made the movement more effective?
- Source C. Were the radicals in a no-win situation: wanting 'numbers' so that 'resistance was hopeless' but withholding any threat of force, avoiding 'breaches of the peace', which might have wrung concessions from the government?

  You should conclude with what you think are the most important reasons, making a judgement about the **extent** to which it was the actions of a harsh, repressive government which explain the failure of the popular movement.

In the style of Edexcel
Answer both parts of the question below:

(a) Explain the methods used by the radicals in their campaign for parliamentary reform. (20 marks)
(b) How effective was the radical campaign for reform in the period from 1815 to 1820? (40 marks)

Exam tips
The cross-references are intended to take you straight to the material that will help you to answer the questions.

(a) In an exam, you should aim to complete question (a) in about 15–20 minutes so no more than a side/100–250 words of writing would be expected. You should use your own knowledge to explain the various methods used:

- the press, e.g. Cobbett's *Political Register* and its influence
- Hampden Clubs and petitioning
- mass meetings like Spa Fields and Peterloo
- also explain the more direct, militant action such as the Blanketeers or Pentrich Rising (pages 18–25).

(b) Question (b) carries the most marks so you need to write a mini-essay. Re-read pages 18–28. When you start writing, you should consider:

- The nature of the campaign, e.g. was it a physical challenge of mass action or the political threat of a demand for political change?
- You need to make a *judgement about the effectiveness* of the methods you identified in your answer to the first question, i.e. the press, the clubs, the mass meetings. Did they win support, strengthen the movement? Did they elicit any concessions from the government or just a clampdown?
- You need to refer to specific incidents and analyse the government's response, e.g. did they force concessions or simply harsh measures from the government? (Spa Fields and use of spies; Peterloo and the Six Acts.)
- You should make a judgement on the impact of the campaign on the government over the period as a whole, e.g. did it cause splits or even panic; did it weaken the government?

  In conclusion, you need to make an overall judgement about whether the campaign brought parliamentary reform nearer. If not, why not? Did the radical movement emerge stronger or learn any lasting lessons for future campaigns?

3 The Tory Government 1820–30: Reform and Crisis

POINTS TO CONSIDER

In the 1820s the economy revived, the protest and unrest subsided and the Tory government embarked on a series of economic and legal reforms that have earned the ministers responsible the name 'Liberal Tories'. Then, after Lord Liverpool retired in 1827, the Tory Party and government fell apart and the Whigs came to power. This chapter covers this period through the following key themes:

- The Liberal Tories 1820–7
- The break-up of the Tory government 1827–30
- The Whigs come to power 1830

Key dates

1822–3		Promotion of 'Liberal Tories' in the government
1823–9		Import duties on many goods reduced
1823		Gaols Act
1824		Repeal of Combination Acts
1826		Reform of the penal code
1827	February	Lord Liverpool resigned
	April	Canning became Prime Minister
	August	Canning died and Goderich became Prime Minister; Wellington, Peel and others left the Cabinet
1828	January	Goderich resigned; Wellington became Prime Minister
	May	Huskisson and other Canningites resigned from government
1829		Metropolitan Police force established Catholic Emancipation Act passed
1830	June	George IV died; William IV came to the throne
	November	Whigs formed a government
1830–1		Swing riots

1 | The Liberal Tories 1820–7

Key question
Who were the Liberal Tories?

In the early 1820s economic conditions improved. Trade increased and unemployment fell. There was a succession of good harvests and bread was cheaper. Not surprisingly, there was less discontent and less social unrest. When Henry Hunt was released from prison in 1822, a few determined radicals celebrated but not the masses.

The Tory government, led by Lord Liverpool, was less threatened by protest and radical politics. Some of the government's harsher policies were relaxed. The 1820s have become known as the years of the 'Liberal Tories'. These so-called Liberal Tories were:

- Sir Robert Peel, who became Home Secretary in 1822
- George Canning, who became Foreign Secretary in 1822
- Frederick Robinson, who became Chancellor of the Exchequer in 1823
- William Huskisson, who became President of the Board of Trade in 1823.

Key date
Lord Liverpool promoted 'Liberal Tories' in the Cabinet: 1822–3

All these men were already experienced Cabinet ministers. Huskisson had been Liverpool's main economic adviser while Peel, in his early thirties, was already regarded as the most able member of Liverpool's team. Peel, Canning and Robinson were all to become Prime Ministers later in their careers. (The fourth, Huskisson, was the first person ever to be killed by a railway train.)

Liverpool promoted these younger men because he needed their administrative experience in running government departments. Above all, he needed their debating skill in the House of Commons. This was important, because Liverpool himself, and several other Cabinet ministers, were peers, so they sat in the House of Lords and could not defend government policy in the Commons. It was even more important at this particular time to have good speakers in key positions as the government had had such a rough ride in Parliament during the Queen Caroline affair in 1820–1 (see page 27) and needed to regain its strength and confidence.

The policies of the Liberal Tories

Key question
How liberal were the Liberal Tories?

In what ways were these newly promoted Cabinet members liberal? There were two major issues on which they were definitely *not* liberal. The first was the question of parliamentary reform: they did not favour it any more than the Prime Minister did. When the Whigs introduced a bill for parliamentary reform in 1822, there was no support from the government and the bill failed by a large majority.

Nor were most of them liberal on the second big issue of the day: that is, religion. Here the big question was whether to extend full political rights to Roman Catholics. Catholics could vote at this time, but they did not have the right to become MPs or hold public office. Lord Liverpool knew that the king and many members of the Tory Party were opposed to any change so he decided that the Cabinet should ignore this issue. Individual ministers could support reform in private but they were not to raise it in Cabinet meetings.

However, the Liberal Tories *were* more liberal on other issues. In the more relaxed political circumstances of the 1820s, they were more responsive to public opinion, especially the 'respectable opinion' of the new, property-owning, industrial and commercial classes. The views of these new **middle classes** were increasingly being voiced by national newspapers like *The Times* and regional newspapers like the *Manchester Guardian* and the *Leeds Mercury*. The Liberal Tories were more willing to listen and respond to the needs of industry and trade. They believed it was important to balance the needs of merchants and industrialists with those of the landowners. In this way, and with the radical threat diminished, they were able to be more liberal than their predecessors had been.

Liverpool and his ministers realised that an increasing proportion of Britain's wealth was now being produced in factories, mills and mines. They also recognised that trade was increasingly important, both for the import of raw materials needed by industry and for the export of manufactured goods. They were keen to encourage this economic growth. They knew that increased prosperity would mean less criticism of the government and less protest across the country. In other words, a strong economy was the key to social and political stability. One area where they were more liberal, and keen to carry out reform, was in trade.

Key term

Middle classes
People below the landowning aristocracy, but who do not do manual labour. Many – manufacturers, merchants, bankers, shopkeepers – made their money from industry and trade. Others were members of the professions, such as lawyers, doctors, teachers.

Economic policy

Liverpool and his ministers, particularly Huskisson and Robinson, believed that Britain's trade was hampered by old and outdated regulations. One example was the Navigation Acts. These had been passed in order to protect British shipping from competition with the Dutch in the seventeenth century. They prevented foreign ships from transporting goods to or from Britain and British colonies so that only British ships could do this. These laws were no longer necessary as Britain was now a much stronger trading nation. The Navigation Acts also restricted trade even more because other countries simply retaliated with their own laws banning British ships from *their* ports.

Key question
Why and how were trade restrictions relaxed?

Reciprocity of Goods Act 1823

In 1823 Huskisson persuaded Parliament to pass the Reciprocity of Goods Act. This allowed the British government to make agreements with other countries whereby Britain would get rid of such restrictions on trade with a particular country if the other country agreed to do the same. This is called a reciprocal, or mutual, arrangement. This would help to reduce the cost of imports, such as raw materials. This was particularly important for the textile industry. This was the fastest growing industry in Britain and it depended on imports of raw cotton from the USA.

The more cotton could be imported, the more cloth could be manufactured. This meant more jobs, more profits and more wealth, especially as the textile industry at this time accounted for 80 per cent of British exports.

Reduction of import duties

Another area of economic reform was **import duties** (or tariffs). There were hundreds of different import duties, charging different amounts of duty on different imported goods. These had been built up over hundreds of years, both to regulate trade and also to raise money for the government. Lord Liverpool and his Chancellor of the Exchequer, Robinson, decided to simplify this complex and muddled collection of duties and to make it more efficient. Above all, they decided to reduce import duties. There were several reasons for this:

- If Britain reduced import duties on foreign goods coming into Britain, other countries might do the same for British goods.
- Britain was now the leading industrial nation. It was producing more industrial goods, often more cheaply, than other countries and the government was confident that Britain would be able to export more of its manufactured goods in a climate of freer trade.
- If import duties on raw materials like cotton were reduced, the textile industry would be stimulated because more, cheaper cotton could be imported and more cotton goods could be produced more cheaply. This industrial growth would lead to greater national prosperity.
- If import duties were reduced, there might be less smuggling as it would not be so profitable.

Key terms

Import duties
Taxes (or tariffs) paid on imported goods.

Free trade
The idea that goods should be traded between countries without any duties (or tariffs) being imposed. Liberal Tory policies moved towards freer trade by reducing import duties.

Key date

Import duties on many goods were reduced: 1823–9

In a series of budgets in the mid-1820s, Robinson slashed duties on imports: he cut duties on manufactured goods from 50 to 20 per cent and on raw materials, such as cotton, wool and coal, from 20 to 10 per cent. Although this might mean less income for the government, he was able to do it because Britain was undergoing an economic revival and trade was growing. In fact, despite lower import duties, government income from this source rose by 64 per cent between 1821 and 1827 because trade increased so much. The Chancellor earned the nickname 'Prosperity' Robinson and the government became more popular than it had ever been.

In many ways these Liberal Tory measures were a continuation of the **free trade** policies that had been started by the Prime Minister William Pitt, before the French wars. By reducing high import duties and getting rid of other restrictions, they certainly helped, like Pitt had done, to make trade more efficient. However, there was one area of trade where any interference with the existing duties raised huge opposition – the Corn Laws.

The Corn Laws

Although the Corn Laws of 1815 (see page 17) were hated by the middle and working classes, most of the landowning classes who dominated Parliament and Liverpool's government resisted any major change to them. Nevertheless, minor adjustments were made. In 1822, even before Huskisson and Robinson were promoted, the Laws were modified so that imports of wheat were allowed when the price reached 70 shillings (£3.50) a quarter (previously, no imports were allowed until the price reached 80 shillings). However, with good harvests and increased wheat production in the 1820s, the price stayed low and never reached this level. Huskisson, who was MP for the city of Liverpool, recognised that cheap bread was good for 'the labouring parts of the community'.

In 1828, a sliding scale was introduced. This meant that wheat could be imported when the price was 60 shillings (£3.00) a quarter, paying a duty that was progressively reduced as the price went up, and could then be imported free of import duty when the price reached 73 shillings (£3.65). These modifications to the Corn Laws, although disliked by many landowning Tory MPs,

Profile: Lord Liverpool 1770–1827

1770	– Born Robert Banks Jenkinson, the son of a political adviser to George III
1790	– Became a Tory MP
1808	– Inherited his father's title to become second Earl of Liverpool (although always known as Lord Liverpool)
1801–12	– Foreign Secretary, then Home Secretary and then Secretary for War
1812–27	– Prime Minister, the longest serving of the nineteenth century
1827	– Suffered a stroke, resigned and died a year later

Lord Liverpool was Prime Minister in the final three years of the war against France. He is associated with the final victory in 1815 and the years of so-called 'repressive' government from 1815 to 1820 (see Chapter 2). Yet he was cautiously reforming: for instance, he would have kept the income tax after the war but Parliament insisted on its removal (page 17). He supported tough laws to deal with the radical agitation after 1815, yet he encouraged 'liberal' reforms when economic conditions improved and prosperity returned in the 1820s.

Liverpool was not a dynamic or inspiring leader, but he was hugely experienced, highly respected and widely trusted. Above all, he appointed capable, younger men like Peel, Huskisson, Robinson and Canning and supported them in their policies. He also kept the balance between the different groups and strong personalities in his Cabinet. The fact that the Tory party split up so spectacularly and so quickly after his death suggests that he had been a unifying and restraining influence on the Tory government. One historian has written: 'Liverpool was certainly the only man who could hold together the Cabinet between 1822 and 1827'.

were comparatively minor changes. All in all, the government was not very 'liberal' on the issue of the Corn Laws.

The meaning of the word' liberal'

The term 'liberal' has been applied to members of the Tory government in the 1820s. It has been used mainly because of their willingness to be more responsive to the new middle classes such as factory and mine owners, merchants and bankers, who became wealthy as a result of the Industrial Revolution. For instance, the Liberal Tories favoured a policy of more free trade that was particularly favoured by industrialists. However, not all of the Tories were equally liberal: Canning privately favoured Catholic Emancipation but Peel was opposed to it even though he did support free trade and reform of the law. None of the Liberal Tories supported parliamentary reform, at least not until the end of the 1820s. The reform of the law, carried out by Peel as Home Secretary, was seen as liberal and this is now examined below.

Reform of the law

Key question
How 'liberal' were Peel's legal reforms?

Another area in which reforms were carried out by Lord Liverpool's government was the law. Crime rates had doubled in the seven years following the end of the wars with France in 1815. Like today, these figures had an alarming effect. A government committee had already been set up in 1819 and had made some recommendations but it was Sir Robert Peel, the Home Secretary from 1823, who steered the subsequent reforms through Parliament. He used his vast knowledge and his debating skill to persuade the MPs that reforms would make the legal system more effective.

Reform of the penal code 1826

Key terms

Penal code
A document, or series of documents, that states what penalties should be awarded for particular offences.

Transportation
It was a common sentence for convicts to be sent to Australia for prison or compulsory labour.

The **penal code** in England was made up of hundreds of different laws which stated what sentences should be administered for which offences. Some of these laws were very old, many of them were overlapping or even contradictory. The whole system was chaotic. What made it even less effective was that many of the sentences were completely inappropriate. For instance, there were over 200 offences that carried the death penalty. Some of them, such as poaching and stealing a sheep, seemed so harsh that juries often acquitted those who were blatantly guilty because they felt that the crime did not deserve hanging. This meant that the law was not respected or enforced.

Peel set out to change this. He wanted to make the law more effective. He wanted the system to work more efficiently. He got rid of many old laws and simplified the whole penal code. He reduced what had been hundreds of different laws to just eight! He cut down the number of offences for which you could be hanged. For many of those offences the penalty would now be **transportation** to Australia. By the late 1820s, over 5000 convicts a year were being transported to prison camps on the far side of the world. Transportation was more humane and it was also a pretty permanent solution.

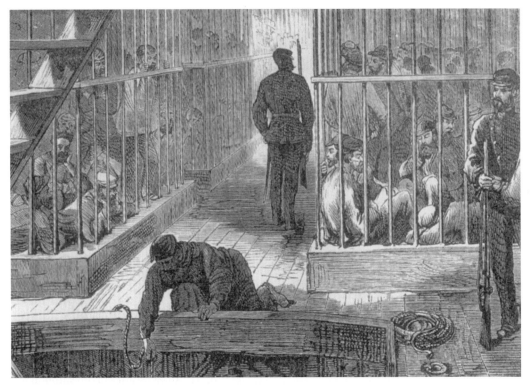

This nineteenth-century drawing shows convicts being transported to Australia. Conditions were so poor that many died during the voyage.

Yet Peel was not a great **humanitarian**: if anything, he wanted the law to be more punitive and to get more people convicted. He believed that if the penalty for stealing a sheep was transportation, then a jury was far more likely to convict a person who they thought was guilty of the offence than if the penalty was hanging. He wanted the whole system to be more efficient and effective. Only in this sense was he a 'liberal'.

The Gaols Act 1823

Another area in which Peel carried out reform was in the running of the gaols (sometimes spelled as 'jails'). Local prisons were often filthy and inhumane. Gaolers were often unpaid and therefore likely to try and extort money from the inmates. The Gaols Act of 1823 obliged each county and large town to maintain a prison, paid for by the local taxes and controlled by the magistrates. It also established a standard system of discipline and inspection and stated that gaolers should be paid and inmates provided with a basic education.

Peel was undoubtedly influenced by the humanitarian reformers who had been campaigning for many years: he certainly wanted a fairer system. However, his motives were largely those of the administrator, keen to establish a uniform and effective system right across the country.

Humanitarian
A person who works for the welfare of all human beings.

Key term

Metropolitan Police Force 1829

Peel is probably best known for establishing the Metropolitan Police in London. Previously, the authorities had to rely on an informal system of part-time, low-paid constables and informers, but this did not prevent rising crime in what was a city of 1.5 million people, ten times more than any other city in Britain. Many people were deeply suspicious of Peel's proposal and saw a new police force as a threat to civil liberties. They associated such a force with some of the more harsh, dictatorial governments on the continent. An earlier attempt to set up a new police force had failed.

As with his reforms of the law, Peel worked hard to gather the evidence and the arguments with which to convince Parliament of the need to establish a professional police force. The new Act established a force of 3000 men, organised in five divisions across the capital. They were deliberately dressed in uniforms that were non-military in appearance and were armed only with truncheons. They soon became known as 'Bobbies' after Robert Peel. In the next few years crime rates in London were brought down and, in the 1830s, police forces were established in other parts of the country.

Repeal of the Combination Acts 1824

Key question
Why were the Combination Acts repealed?

Key terms

Combination Acts
Laws passed to ban the formation of trade unions, or combinations, of working men.

Picketing
Standing outside a factory or other workplace to discourage people from going to work.

In 1799 and 1800, at the height of the war against France, the government had banned trade unions, or combinations, of working men. The **Combination Acts**, as they were called, were passed because the government was afraid of men joining together to form unions that might challenge the government. This was a time of war and there was great fear of plots and conspiracies.

Twenty years later a campaign was launched by a radical politician, Francis Place, to repeal the Combination Laws and thus make it legal to form trade unions. He argued that it was safer to allow working men to form unions and to bargain with their employers over wages and working conditions than it was for unions to remain illegal and thus have to become secretive, underground organisations.

Although the government did not actively support the campaign for repeal, they did not oppose it either. By the mid-1820s, Britain was more prosperous and peaceful so there was less fear of trade unions. In 1824, the Combination Acts were repealed. Thousands of men formed unions, especially in the industrial areas of the North and the Midlands. Furthermore, with the economy booming and a shortage of labour, the workers were in a stronger position to call for higher wages and threaten strike action if their demands were not met. Sure enough, there was a rash of strikes. This alarmed most MPs and, in 1825, an amending law was passed which banned the use of force or intimidation. It became an offence to *force* a man to become a union member or join in a strike. This effectively made strikes and **picketing** illegal. Thus, trade unions were now allowed but their powers were restricted.

Summary diagram: The Liberal Tories 1820–7

Promotions to key posts in 1822–3
Peel, Canning, Robinson, Huskisson

Trade reform
Lower import duties

Law reform
Better gaols (1823) • Fewer capital offences (1826) • Metropolitan Police (1829)

Repeal of Combination Acts 1824

2 | The Break-up of the Tory Government 1827–30

In 1827, when Lord Liverpool retired, the Tories had been in government almost uninterrupted for over 40 years. Yet in the next three years they were to split apart and fall from power. The speed with which this happened astounded people at the time as well as historians since then. The biggest single issue on which the government divided was **Catholic Emancipation** but there were also many personal rivalries and political tensions within the government.

Under Lord Liverpool most property owners, whether they owned their own land, houses or businesses, had supported the Tory government's opposition to political reform (such as extending the right to vote), while supporting its cautious economic reform. The most controversial issue of the day was Catholic Emancipation and Liverpool knew that the king, most of his own Tory Party and much of the voting public were opposed to it. For this reason, he made it an 'open' question for members of his government. This meant that they could hold their own opinions as long as they did not voice them publicly. In effect, Liverpool was ignoring the issue in order to maintain the unity of his government. But it was only a short-term solution and, when Liverpool left government, it flared up.

Liverpool retired in February 1827 and George Canning was expected to succeed him as Prime Minister. Liverpool had regarded him as his successor and Canning was widely agreed to be a highly talented man and a very successful foreign secretary. But his very success and the way he paraded it made him enemies. He was a flamboyant figure and he deliberately sought publicity, courting the press and letting them know of his successes. In many ways he was more like a modern politician.

Key question
Why did the Tory government disintegrate between 1827 and 1830?

Catholic Emancipation Allowing Roman Catholics the right to become MPs or to hold other public office.

Key term

Liverpool had a stroke and retired: February 1827

Canning became Prime Minister; Wellington, Peel and others left the Cabinet: April 1827

Key dates

This was resented by some of his colleagues. Snobbery came into it as well: he was the son of an actress at a time when birth and breeding were regarded as important. Some saw the way he flaunted his achievements as vulgar. But, above all, what made him enemies in the Cabinet was his sympathy for Catholic Emancipation.

Canning becomes Prime Minister, April 1827

When the king asked Canning to be Prime Minister and to form a government, the Duke of Wellington, Robert Peel and nearly half of the Tory Cabinet refused to serve under him. These men came to be regarded as the 'Protestant' Tories because of their opposition to Catholic Emancipation. So Canning approached the leading Whigs. Several of them, especially Earl Grey, the Whig leader, refused to serve under him but three of them accepted Cabinet posts. (One member of the Whig party said that Canning as Prime Minister had 'dissected both Whigs and Tories'. This was a bit of an exaggeration but it was true that one man and one issue had split opinion *across* party lines.)

It took Canning three months to form a government, which he finally did in April 1827, and then he died four months later! The stress and strain of government, together with lung and liver problems, had exhausted him. The king now turned to Robinson, who had been Lord Liverpool's Chancellor of the Exchequer. Robinson was now Viscount Goderich, having been made a member of the House of Lords a few months before. He was experienced in government, but was a weak leader and both the Whigs and the '**Canningites**' deserted him. He resigned in January 1828.

Key term

Canningites
Political allies and followers of George Canning. They were only a small group but they included two future Prime Ministers, Lord Melbourne and Lord Palmerston.

Key dates

Canning died; Goderich became Prime Minister: August 1827

Goderich resigned and Wellington formed a government: January 1828

Huskisson and other Canningites resigned from the government: May 1828

Repeal of the Test and Corporation Acts 1828

In the seventeenth century, after the English Civil War, the government had been keen to make the Church of England strong and dominant, a necessary support for the monarchy. The Church of England was the official State Church and the king was its head. The Test and Corporation Acts, passed in 1661 and 1673, imposed a test for those holding public office: you had to be an Anglican (a member of the Church of England). Since then, these laws had often been ignored, especially for Nonconformists. These people were Protestants but they were not Anglican. Instead, they were Baptists, Quakers, Presbyterians, Methodists and so on.

In 1828, the Whigs introduced a Bill into Parliament to repeal, or overturn, the Test and Corporation Acts and to grant full rights to Nonconformists. The Tory government did not oppose this and the repeal was passed. Now, however, it became far more difficult to justify the exclusion of Catholics from their civil rights. Now the argument in favour of Catholic Emancipation was stronger.

The Duke of Wellington as Prime Minister, January 1828

Wellington became Prime Minister: January 1828

Key date

The king was now forced back into depending on the 'Protestant' Tories, those who opposed Catholic Emancipation. He summoned the Duke of Wellington, confident that the military hero who had defeated Napoleon could form a 'strong government'. At first it looked as if Wellington had restored the stability of Liverpool's government. He even brought the Canningites back into the Cabinet. However, he never forgave them for weakening the Tory government, as he saw it, by bringing the Whigs into government in 1827. He could never trust them and there were endless disputes in Cabinet. One of these concerned the new Corn Law of 1828 (see page 36). Although it seemed like a minor adjustment of the 1815 Corn Laws, it still alienated many landowning Tories.

Key question
Why did Wellington's appointment cause further splits in the Tory Party?

Another cause of disagreement was parliamentary reform. After the general election of 1826 two small parliamentary constituencies had been found guilty of electoral corruption and it was decided that they should lose their seats in Parliament. Most of the Cabinet wanted to transfer the seats to rural areas, but the Canningites wanted the seats to go to the industrial cities of Manchester and Leeds. The Canningites did not get their way and, although it was only a minor issue, their leader, William Huskisson, offered to resign in May 1828. Wellington immediately accepted his resignation. The other Canningites followed Huskisson out of the Cabinet. The government thus lost several skilled debaters in Parliament and, with Wellington sitting in the Lords, the government was now very dependent on Peel to give a lead in the Commons.

Party loyalties were now very fluid. The Canningites sided with the Whigs against what was seen as a government of **Ultra Tories**. The Canningites, as well as being sympathetic to Catholic Emancipation, now began to support Whig proposals for parliamentary reform. The issue of Catholic Emancipation and, to a lesser extent, of parliamentary reform, as well as personal clashes and rivalries, was bringing about a major shift in party loyalties and alliances. We must now examine why the issue of Catholic Emancipation was so divisive.

Ultra Tories
Hardline Tories who resisted any constitutional change, especially the granting of political rights to Catholics.

Key term

Catholic Emancipation

The question of Catholic Emancipation was as controversial in the 1820s as the issue of immigration or Britain's position in Europe is today. It was a sensitive issue that aroused very strong emotions. But what *was* it? How did it originate?

Key question
Why was the issue of Catholic Emancipation so controversial?

Since the sixteenth century, most of Britain had been Protestant. Under Henry VIII, in the 1530s, England had broken away from the Catholic Church. This had led to the establishment of a specifically English, or Anglican, Church with the monarch at the head. Catholics came to be distrusted, especially when they were seen as a threat to England's security and independence. For instance, at the time of the Spanish Armada in 1588, when the

Catholic forces of the Spanish king attempted to invade England, some English Catholics were suspected of plotting to overthrow Queen Elizabeth. Later, in 1605, a group of Catholics (Guy Fawkes is the best known of them) hatched a spectacular terrorist plot: they planned to blow up the king, his ministers and all the MPs at the opening of Parliament. Then, in 1688–9, the Catholic King James II was replaced by the Protestant King William. It was at this time that laws were passed to prevent a Catholic from ever becoming monarch and to exclude Catholics from becoming MPs or holding any other public office (such as being a judge or magistrate).

However, one part of Britain remained solidly Catholic and that was Ireland. All of Ireland was ruled by Britain and many of the biggest landlords and government officials in Ireland were English (or Scottish). Many Irish people resented this.

Act of Union 1800

In 1798 there was a revolt against British rule in Ireland. After it had been put down the British government decided to bring Ireland under closer control. The **Act of Union**, in 1800, abolished the Irish parliament in Dublin. From now onwards, the 100 Irish MPs had to travel to England and sit in the Parliament in London. The loss of their own parliament angered many of the Irish. What made it even worse was that Catholics, who formed the majority of the population, were still not allowed to become MPs. They could vote but they could not sit in Parliament.

Daniel O'Connell and the Catholic Association

By the middle of the 1820s there was a mass movement in Ireland demanding full political rights for Catholics. This movement, the Catholic Association, was led by Daniel O'Connell. The Association organised huge demonstrations and meetings. Governing Ireland became increasingly difficult. How would the government in London respond?

Many Whigs and some Tories favoured Catholic Emancipation. After all, Britain was much more secure now that she had defeated France and many of Britain's best soldiers were Catholic. But most Tories and many British people still felt that Catholics were not completely loyal. After all, they still belonged to a foreign, alien Church and the head of that Church was the Pope, not the monarch. The Church of England was the official Church and many felt that the unity of Church and State, both headed by the Crown, would be weakened if Catholics were granted full political rights. It would be overturning hundreds of years of history. It is hard for us, in the twenty-first century, to understand how strong were feelings on this matter of religion. (It is similar to some people's feelings today about keeping the pound or over immigration.)

The County Clare election, July 1828

The issue of Catholic Emancipation came to a head in July 1828. The Duke of Wellington appointed an Irish MP, Vesey Fitzgerald, to the Cabinet. This required a by-election so that the constituents could decide whether they wanted to have the same MP once he had become a government minister. Fitzgerald was MP for County Clare in Ireland and, in the election, Daniel O'Connell, leader of the Catholic Association, decided to stand against him. O'Connell was a Catholic so he would not be able to take his seat in Parliament but he won a huge majority. How would the government react? Wellington knew, from the reports of government officials in Ireland, that there was a danger of a complete breakdown of British rule. Government officials, even when helped by thousands of troops, were finding it almost impossible to maintain law and order. There was a threat of civil war in which the vast majority of Irish might side with the Catholic Association and refuse to obey British government officials in Ireland.

The Duke made up his mind: an Act for Catholic Emancipation would have to be passed in order to preserve British rule in Ireland. Wellington, like Peel, had been seen as a 'Protestant' Tory but he was confident that he could persuade the king not to be obstructive and that his own prestige was such that he could persuade the House of Lords to pass it. The biggest problem was going to be the House of Commons because most Tories were opposed to Catholic Emancipation. Here Peel, who now believed that only Emancipation could prevent open rebellion against British rule in Ireland, would have to steer the Bill through. The government knew that the Whigs would support the measure but the great challenge was to persuade as many Tories as possible to pass it so as to prevent too big a split in the Tory Party.

The effect of Catholic Emancipation on the Tory Party

In the event, the Act was passed in April 1829. A total of 173 Tory MPs voted against it. These Ultra Tories believed that Catholic Emancipation was an assault on the British constitution, a threat to national stability and a betrayal of Tory principles. To them, the very foundations of British society had been undermined. Many Tory MPs never forgave Peel, while the Marquis of Winchilsea even challenged Wellington to a duel for surrendering to Catholic pressure. There was also widespread opposition in the country at large, especially in cities such as Liverpool and Glasgow where there were many Irish immigrants. Cartoons, like the one opposite, reflected popular opinion.

The Tory Party was now split three ways: the Canningites, soon to be allied to the Whigs, the Ultras and those loyal to Wellington and Peel. A year later, in June 1830, the death of the king necessitated a general election. Against a background of recent poor harvests, rising unemployment and a revival of radical demands for reform, the government suffered further losses in the elections and still had no firm majority in Parliament.

Key question
Why did the County Clare election lead to the passing of Catholic Emancipation?

Key question
What impact did Catholic Emancipation have on the Tory Party?

Key dates

Catholic Emancipation Act passed: April 1829

George IV died; William IV came to throne: June 1830

This contemporary cartoon pokes fun at Wellington for passing Catholic Emancipation. It shows the Duke and his allies pulling down the steeple of an Anglican church, much to the enjoyment of a Catholic priest in the foreground.

When the new Parliament met in November 1830, Wellington tried to win back the support of the Ultras. He made a speech in which he said he saw no need to consider any change to the parliamentary system: 'the legislature [Parliament] and the system of representation possesses the full and entire confidence of the country.'

Wellington seemed to be blocking any discussion of reform yet, at this time, there was increasing debate, both inside and outside Parliament, about the need for some kind of reform. The Whigs were pushing for parliamentary reform and they were now stronger and more confident. They had the support of the Canningites who were experienced in government and, in King William IV, they had a monarch who was not opposed to them as King George IV had been. For the first time in many years, the Whigs looked like a realistic alternative to the Tory government. When the Ultra Tories, still seeking revenge against Wellington and Peel, joined the Whigs and the Canningites to defeat the government in Parliament, Wellington resigned and the new king invited Earl Grey, the Whig leader, to form a government.

After dominating the government for over 40 years, the Tory Party had disintegrated and fallen from power. As the historian Norman Gash wrote in 1996:

> by 1827–30, the divisions [in the government] had become too open, its resources too restricted, and its political aims too limited to provide an adequate political channel for the forces of change in British and Irish society.

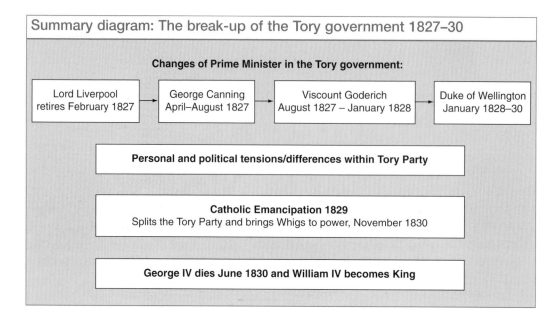

3 | The Whigs Come to Power 1830

The new government was a coalition (or combination) of Whigs and Canningite Tories. Two of the latter were appointed to very senior posts in the Cabinet: Lord Palmerston became Foreign Secretary and Lord Melbourne became Home Secretary. The Whigs in the Cabinet were nearly all landowning aristocrats. In fact, all but four members of the Cabinet sat in the House of Lords.

The most notable Whig member of the House of Commons was Henry Brougham, who had recently campaigned for parliamentary reform and had become the first non-Yorkshireman to be elected for the county of Yorkshire for 300 years. Brougham was a known radical but, on the whole, the new government did not look like a radical, reforming administration. Moreover, it soon showed it could be just as harsh in dealing with violent protest as any Tory government. The cause of this was the so-called **'Swing' riots**.

The Swing riots 1830–1

In the summer of 1830 riots erupted in many rural parts of southern and eastern England. The rioters were agricultural labourers and rural craftsmen and the disturbances were called the Swing riots because the name Captain Swing appeared at the bottom of threatening letters sent to landowners and other local leaders. The causes varied from area to area but major factors were:

- poor harvests in 1829 and 1830
- rising prices and population
- a shortage of jobs available in the countryside.

Key term

Swing riots
Rural riots in the south and east of England in 1830–1. The mythical leader of the riots was 'Captain Swing'.

Key question
How did the Whig government respond to the Swing riots?

Although the unrest was not politically inspired or organised, the targets were often deliberately chosen. Common targets were:

- new threshing machines, which threatened the jobs of farm workers
- the property of farmers who had reduced labourers' wages
- magistrates, who gave out what were seen as harsh sentences for poaching, sometimes received threatening letters.

There were 1400 reported cases between the summer of 1830 and the autumn of 1831 of what came to be known as the Swing riots. Lord Melbourne was as tough as any Home Secretary had been in Liverpool's government. He encouraged magistrates to give out harsh sentences, used troops where necessary and set up special commissions to try offenders. Not a single person was killed in the Swing riots but thousands of rioters were arrested and put on trial: altogether, 19 were executed and over 450 were transported for life.

Although the riots were not linked to demands for reform of Parliament, they undoubtedly contributed to a rise in the political temperature. There were several other developments that also played a part in this. In July 1830 there was another French revolution. It was not as violent or as large scale as in 1789, but it led to the downfall of the Bourbon monarchy and the establishment of a new king. Meanwhile, in several cities across Britain, **political unions**, or societies, re-appeared. This revival was partly a response to deteriorating economic conditions but was also a result of the recent election and the events in France.

Political unions

The most notable political society was the Birmingham Political Union (BPU), led by Thomas Attwood. Its first meeting attracted a crowd of 15,000. It aimed to achieve reform of Parliament through the pressure exerted by a 'general political union of the lower and the middle classes of the people'. Attwood saw what success the Catholic Association had had as a result of attracting mass membership and being well organised. He said: 'The Irish people have lately obtained a glorious and bloodless victory.' Perhaps reform of Parliament might be achieved in the same way?

Not all societies attracted the same mixture of middle and working class support as the BPU. The Metropolitan Political Union, founded in London by Henry Hunt, was dominated by artisans and craftsmen, many of whom had been active in radical politics in the years after 1815 (see pages 18–27). Some societies were decidedly middle class in composition, made up of merchants, lawyers and businessmen who were keen to make government more responsive to the needs of trade and industry. Political societies were formed in Manchester, Leeds, Sheffield and many other towns and cities. Their membership and aims varied but they all added to the pressure **'out of doors'** for reform of the political system. Meanwhile, in Parliament, MPs increasingly recognised that continued resistance to demands for reform would only provoke violence. The Whigs were not as out

Key question
What were the aims of the political unions?

Key terms

Political unions
Popular organisations created to campaign for reform of Parliament.

'Out of doors'
Used to describe political activity beyond Parliament, e.g. agitation 'out of doors' meant agitation in the country as a whole.

of touch as the Duke of Wellington had been and, in March 1831, they introduced a bill for the reform of Parliament in the House of Commons. The 'struggle for reform' is the subject of the next chapter.

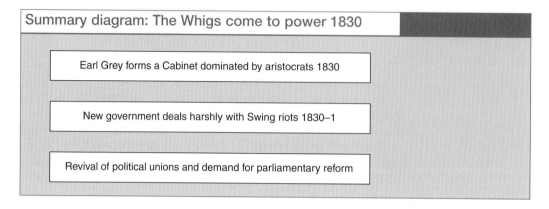

Summary diagram: The Whigs come to power 1830

Earl Grey forms a Cabinet dominated by aristocrats 1830

New government deals harshly with Swing riots 1830–1

Revival of political unions and demand for parliamentary reform

Study Guide

In the style of AQA

Study the following source material and then answer the questions that follow.

Source A

Adapted from: Norman Gash '1812–30', in How Tory Governments Fall, *Anthony Seldon, 1996.*

What is surprising is not how little but how much Lord Liverpool's ministry had been able to achieve in its fifteen years of office. But by 1827–30, the divisions [in the Tory government] had become too open, its resources too restricted, and its political aims too limited to provide an adequate political channel for the forces of political change in British and Irish society.

Source B

Adapted from: James Grant, a parliamentary reporter at the time, commenting on Wellington's period as Prime Minister from 1828 to 1830.

Not only did the noble Duke conduct his government safely through the storms and tempests of the period, but at the very moment he made his ill-judged declaration against all reform [in November 1830], it seemed to be resting more securely than ever.

Source C

From: 'Corn, Catholics and the Constitution: The Tory Crisis of 1827–30' by Graham Goodlad, in History Review, *September 2002.*

Between 1827 and 1830 the Tory Party failed to produce effective leadership at a time of exceptional strain and controversy. It failed to resolve in a united way the central strategic problem of the period: whether to meet the forces of change with a straightforward posture of resistance, or to adapt itself in a more flexible and creative manner.

(a) **Use Source A and your own knowledge**
Explain the significance of the year 1827 in the context of the Tory government in the 1820s. (3 marks)

(b) **Use Source B and your own knowledge**
How useful is this source as evidence about the role of Wellington as Prime Minister? (7 marks)

(c) **Use Sources A, B and C and your own knowledge**
'Catholic Emancipation was the most important factor in the disintegration of the Tory government between 1827 and 1830.' Explain whether you agree or disagree with this statement. (15 marks)

Exam tips

The cross-references are intended to take you straight to the material that will help you to answer the questions.

You will have about 40–45 minutes in which to answer all three questions. The number of marks allotted for each sub-question is an indication of how long to spend on each separate question. Suggestion: spend over half the time on the last question as it carries more marks than the other two combined. Therefore, you should allow about 25 minutes for **(c)**.

(a) For question **(a)** you need to make use of both the source and your own knowledge. The main significance is that 1827 is the year when Liverpool retired from government. You need to explain briefly (four or five sentences at most) what followed:

- the personal tensions and rivalries ('the divisions' referred to in the source)
- the disagreements over policy (explain 'its political aims too limited' from the source, e.g. had the government run out of policies on which the its members could agree?).
  You might show how these differences all came out into the open once Liverpool left the scene and thus made the establishment of a stable government very difficult (pages 40–5).

(b) With question **(b)** you should comment on the usefulness of this as a primary source, e.g. would the author have first-hand evidence? If so, does it seem to be a balanced, objective view? Here your own knowledge will help you arrive at your judgement. Re-read pages 42–5. Does what you have read cause you to disagree with the author's view? If so, you must explain why you disagree and whether this might lead you to have doubts about the usefulness of the source. And, even if you disagree with the author's viewpoint or think it biased, you might find his views useful as a reflection of how some sections of public opinion viewed the Duke. Remember: no source is wholly useless and a biased one can definitely have its uses.

(c) Question **(c)** requires a mini-essay in which you analyse the effects of Catholic Emancipation on the Tory party and government and compare those effects with other factors. You should re-read pages 42–5 in order to:

- understand why, and to what extent, the issue of Catholic Emancipation caused splits within the party and contributed to the instability of the government
- understand the other factors and here you should make reference to the sources
- explain 'the divisions … resources too limited … political aims too limited' referred to in Source A
- explain Wellington's 'ill-judged declaration' from Source B and assess its effects
- examine the 'failure of effective leadership at a time of exceptional strain and controversy' and how the Tory Party addressed what Source C sees as the 'central strategic problem of the period'.

  You should use your own knowledge to explain and explore factors not referred to in the sources or your analysis of them. Finally, you need to weigh up what you see as the main reasons for the disintegration of the party and government and arrive at a balanced judgement. In your conclusion, you should definitely refer to the divisive effects of Catholic Emancipation, as it is specifically referred to in the question, even if you do not think it is the most significant reason for the disintegration of the party or government.

In the style of Edexcel

Answer both parts of the question below.

(a) In what ways were the years 1822–3 a turning point in the policies of the Tory government from 1820 to 1830? (20 marks)

(b) To what extent were the domestic policies of Lord Liverpool's government from 1820 to 1827 liberal? (40 marks)

Exam tips

The cross-references are intended to take you straight to the material that will help you to answer the questions.

(a) For question **(a)**, a couple of paragraphs, perhaps seven or eight sentences, should be enough. You need to use your own knowledge to:

- identify the changes that took place in 1822–3
- explain the ways in which they constituted a turning point, e.g. did the changes in membership of the Cabinet lead to a change in government style or its policy?
- You should focus on what you see as the *most* significant changes, making brief comparisons between policies before and after 1822–3 (pages 33–45).

(b) Question **(b)** carries more marks so you should spend about 40 minutes on it. It requires an essay of a few hundred words. You should spend a few minutes planning it.

- Start by listing the key policies down the left-hand side of a page, e.g. (i) economic policies, particularly concerning trade and import duties; (ii) changes in the law and in running gaols; (iii) police; and (iv) Corn Laws.
- Then make a few notes, on the right, about the ways in which each of the policies were, or were not, liberal. You might refer back to the section entitled 'The meaning of the word liberal' on page 37.
- Now compose your answer. You should also identify the areas in which the government were not reforming (e.g. on questions of religion and extension of the franchise) and in which they were no more liberal than they had been before 1820.
- Conclude by drawing out the key policies and their chief characteristics, and make your overall *judgement about the extent* to which they were liberal (pages 33–9).

4 The Whigs and the Reform Bill 1830–2

POINTS TO CONSIDER

When the Whigs came to power in 1830 they decided to reform Parliament and the way it was elected. It was to be a long political struggle and led to the passing of the Reform Act of 1832. The reasons for reform and the passage of the Bill through Parliament are examined in this chapter through the themes:

- The unreformed parliamentary system
- Support for reform
- The Reform Bill in the House of Commons 1830–1
- The king, the Lords and the country 1831–2

Key dates

1830	November	Whig government was appointed
1831	March	First Reform Bill introduced and later rejected
	May	General election
	June	Second Reform Bill introduced
	September	Second Bill passed by the Commons
	October	House of Lords rejected the second Bill
		Riots in several cities
	December	Whig government introduced a third Reform Bill
1832	May 7	House of Lords' committee rejected the Bill
		Whig government resigned
	May 14	Wellington failed to form government
		Whigs returned to power
	June	King persuaded Lords to pass the Bill

Key question
What was the parliamentary electoral system like?

1 | The Unreformed Parliamentary System

In 1815 there were 658 members of Parliament. Today the number is 646. Like today, the country was divided up into **constituencies**: that is, areas in which MPs were elected and sent to Parliament, to sit in the House of Commons. But there the similarities end.

The first major difference to today is that most constituencies returned two members to Parliament (i.e. they were not single-member constituencies). Secondly, these constituencies were of two types: the *county* seats and the *borough* seats. In England, there were 82 county seats and 403 borough seats. There were also two seats each for the ancient universities of Oxford and Cambridge.

Constituencies
Areas into which the country was divided up for elections. Most constituencies returned two MPs to Parliament.

Table 4.1: Number of seats in the House of Commons in 1815

	England	Wales	Scotland	Ireland	Total
County seats	82	12	30	64	188
Borough seats	403	12	15	35	465
University seats	4	0	0	1	5
Total	489	24	45	100	658

This system of county and borough seats had grown up over many centuries. It originated in the Middle Ages when the king called up two knights from every shire (or county) and two burgesses (townspeople) from every borough to make up the House of Commons in Parliament. The counties, or shires (Bedfordshire, Berkshire, Buckinghamshire, etc.), were largely rural. The boroughs were mainly country towns and ports: they had become boroughs when the king gave them the right to send an MP to Parliament. This meant that towns that had been important in medieval times had MPs to represent them while new industrial towns like Manchester and Leeds had no MPs.

Who could vote?

In 1831 the total population of England, Scotland and Wales was 16 million. For the whole of the United Kingdom, including Ireland, it was 24 million. Only a small minority of men, and no women, had the right to vote. Historians estimate that less than half a million men were entitled to vote. This was certainly less than five per cent of the total population. In the counties all men who owned freehold property worth 40 shillings (£2) a year could vote. These people were known as '**forty shilling freeholders**'. In Scottish counties, the right to vote was much more restricted: you had to own property worth £100, so only 4500 men, out of a total population of over two million, could vote.

In the boroughs there was not a uniform or consistent franchise (voting qualification). Instead there was a huge variety of franchises. The five main types are summarised in the box.

Forty shilling freeholders
People who owned land or property worth 40 shillings (£2) a year.

> ## Voting qualifications in borough constituencies
>
> ### Scot and Lot boroughs
> All adult males who paid local taxes, such as rates for the relief of the poor, could vote.
>
> ### Potwalloper boroughs
> All men who occupied a house ('who had a family and boiled a pot') could vote. These were constituencies with the biggest electorates, and the best-known example was Preston, where the radical Henry Hunt was MP.
>
> ### Burgage boroughs
> All men who owned burgages (ancient plots of land or other property) could vote.
>
> ### Corporation boroughs
> Only members of the local town council (or corporation) could vote.
>
> ### Freeman boroughs
> All men who had been granted the title of 'freeman' could vote. This status could be inherited from one's parents.

Key terms

Nominee
Someone put forward for election. Over 200 MPs were nominated by an aristocratic patron who sat in the Lords. In other words, members of the House of Lords had huge control over the composition of the Commons. Often nominees were sons, younger brothers, cousins or friends of the family.

Pocket borough
A constituency that was in the control, hence the pocket, of a particular patron, usually a large landowner. The majority were controlled by Tories.

As shown in the box, there were some boroughs, such as Preston, where almost all men had the vote. There were others, large towns such as Norwich and Nottingham or big seaports such as Bristol and Liverpool, which had several thousand voters. But many boroughs had very small numbers of men who were entitled to vote.

What were pocket boroughs?

In some of these boroughs with only a small electorate, the biggest landowner (or local businessmen) in the area had huge influence and was able to get himself or his **nominee** elected. These boroughs were known as '**pocket boroughs**' as the landowners were seen to have them in their pockets. There were various ways in which this could be done. The voters may have voted for the landowner because they were his tenants or their jobs depended on being employed by him. Such a prominent local figure was often the local magistrate and that might be another reason to keep on his right side! Sometimes, the electors were happy to be bought out and would sell their votes for as high a price as they could get. Votes could be sold for as much as £10, equivalent today to over £500.

What were rotten boroughs?

In some extreme cases there were only 10 or 20 voters. This might be because what had been a town in the Middle Ages had

Key question
Why did pocket and rotten boroughs exist?

Rotten borough
A borough with few or no constituents yet which returned at least one MP to Parliament.

now decayed and contained very few inhabitants. For example, the borough of Dunwich on the east coast of England had virtually disappeared under the sea after hundreds of years of coastal erosion so that only a few houses were left. Old Sarum, in Wiltshire, largely consisted of a number of mounds, ditches and castle remains. It had only seven voters. These extreme examples were known as 'rotten boroughs'.

Over 50 constituencies had fewer than 50 voters each. In constituencies like these, with very few voters, boroughs could be bought and sold. They came to be seen as the property of powerful 'patrons' or the government. The borough of Gatton was sold for £90,000 in 1801 and changed hands again in 1830 for £180,000, which would be equivalent to about £9 million today.

What were elections like?

Elections were very different from today. For a start, they lasted for several days. This was to give everyone time to get to the **polling station**. In a large county such as Yorkshire, it might take several hours to get to the county town of York to cast your vote, so several days were allowed. But the most striking difference is that voting was open: there was no **secret ballot**. Instead, you voted by show of hands. This obviously meant that you might be pressurised: if the local landowner or his supporters were there to see how you voted, you might feel that you had to vote for him or his nominee. After all, your livelihood may depend on him. Historians now believe that about 25 per cent of county electors came under the direct influence of their landlords.

Polling station
A place for voting.

Secret ballot
Casting a vote in secret, as is done today.

If such influence did not work, the candidates could bribe the electors with food, drink and entertainment at election time. Electors could be provided with transport to get to the polling station, especially if they lived some distance away, and they might be put up for the night.

Since the elections lasted for several days, an election could have the atmosphere of a carnival. Elections could be boisterous, sometimes riotous. There were colourful processions, with banners and placards. Insults, and sometimes missiles, were thrown. And not only the electors were involved. Those who did not have the vote could still be employed to whip up support for a particular candidate or to put pressure on those who were likely to vote for the opposing candidate. If voters could not be relied on to vote in the desired way, they could be 'cooped': that is, kidnapped and kept drunk until the election was over.

Why were some elections not contested?

In many constituencies there was no contest at election time. The winner was decided beforehand and no election took place. There were several reasons for this. First, the patron, or owner, of a pocket borough often had no opponent and both the seats went to his nominees. In effect, the seat in Parliament was *owned* by the local leader. As we have seen, seats in Parliament could actually be bought. Many leading members of the government first got into

This engraving of 1754–5 by William Hogarth shows the violence and excitement of an election. It may be exaggerated, like a modern cartoon, but can it still be useful to a historian?

Parliament this way. When the industrialist Robert Peel bought a country estate at Tamworth in Staffordshire, he effectively bought a seat in Parliament. His son, also called Robert, succeeded him as MP for Tamworth and went on to lead the Tories and become Prime Minister.

Even if no one family controlled the constituency or the parliamentary seat, a deal might be done between two leading families so that each took one seat in Parliament. In the 1830 general election, there was not a single contest in Wales; no Welshman had the chance to vote that year.

Support for the old system

The old electoral system strikes us now as chaotic, corrupt and unfair. So how could anyone defend it? One argument was that the very different types of voting qualifications gave a wide variety of people the vote. For example, it was not only the rich who could vote: in the borough of Westminster, which had a large electorate, 12,000 were entitled to vote and many craftsmen and traders did so. In the counties, the 'forty shilling freeholder' franchise included many farmers and not just the biggest landowners. In the county of Yorkshire, for instance, there was an electorate of over 20,000.

Many argued that, even if not all men had the vote, all the different interests were represented. For example, in a port such as Liverpool, the merchants were said to represent the interests of the sailors and the dockworkers while, in the countryside, the

Key question
How could anyone defend the old electoral system?

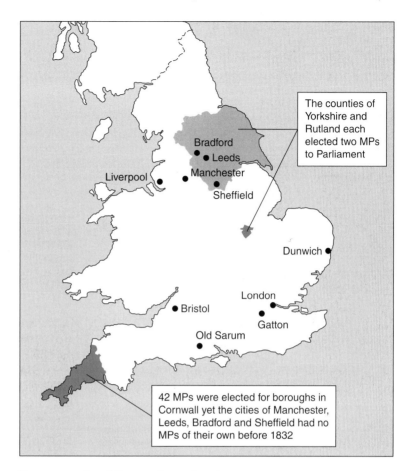

The counties of Yorkshire and Rutland each elected two MPs to Parliament

42 MPs were elected for boroughs in Cornwall yet the cities of Manchester, Leeds, Bradford and Sheffield had no MPs of their own before 1832

The geography of the unreformed system.

landowners had the best interests of their tenants in mind and thus represented all members of the agricultural interest. This was called 'virtual representation'.

Another feature that is difficult for us in modern Britain to appreciate is that this was a very **deferential** society: many people looked up to the local leader. Many voted for him out of traditional respect or simply because they had always done so. They might feel it was in their own best interests to support their local leader's politics. This does not mean to say that they would follow their leader unwillingly. In 1830, Lord Penrhyn spent £30,000 on bribes to the electors of Liverpool but his opponent was elected. A year later, in the 1831 election, thousands of voters defied their traditional leaders and voted for the candidates who supported parliamentary reform; the Tories, who opposed reform, lost nearly all the county seats.

Even the pocket or rotten boroughs were defended by some on the grounds that they had enabled talented men to rise to the top while still young. For example, Canning and Peel had both entered Parliament in such constituencies.

A further argument in defence of the electoral system was that it had lasted for hundreds of years, so why change it? It had

Key term

Deferential
Showing respect for people, in this case for those of a higher class.

served Britain well, it was said. By 1815 Britain was the most advanced industrial nation, with the largest navy in the world and a huge overseas trading empire. Furthermore, it had avoided the violence and killings of revolutionary France. So why challenge this stability and wealth by changing the electoral system?

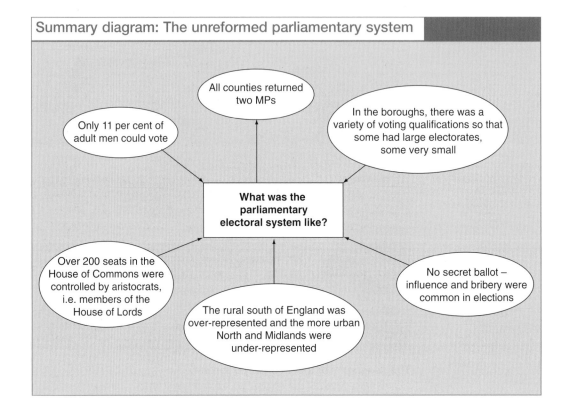

Summary diagram: The unreformed parliamentary system

- All counties returned two MPs
- Only 11 per cent of adult men could vote
- In the boroughs, there was a variety of voting qualifications so that some had large electorates, some very small
- **What was the parliamentary electoral system like?**
- Over 200 seats in the House of Commons were controlled by aristocrats, i.e. members of the House of Lords
- The rural south of England was over-represented and the more urban North and Midlands were under-represented
- No secret ballot – influence and bribery were common in elections

2 | Support for Reform

Key question
Why was there growing demand for reform?

Although many people defended the old system, there had been growing demands for parliamentary reform since the late eighteenth century. Every year petitions were submitted to Parliament: these could be signed by both electors and non-electors. Occasionally the House of Commons debated them in some detail, at other times they spared little time to consider them. Sometimes, the petitions called for a rotten borough to lose its parliamentary seat and for the spare seat to be given to a new industrial town; at other times, the petitions called for a more sweeping reform, such as extending the voting qualification or for a wholesale redistribution of seats from small boroughs with tiny electorates to the big, new towns in the industrial North and Midlands.

During the Napoleonic Wars, from 1793 to 1815, the calls for reform had quietened down, partly because of government action to stifle such demands and partly because of a patriotic sense of duty to concentrate on winning the war. But after the end of the war, in 1815, the reform agitation was re-ignited and attracted increasing support. One of the main reasons for this was that Britain was now an increasingly industrialised nation in which the new middle classes – factory owners and bankers, merchants and shopkeepers – were demanding more of a say in the government of the country. Above all, these people highlighted the fact that the largely rural south of England was over-represented in the House of Commons and the more densely populated industrial areas of the North and Midlands were very under-represented. A few examples will illustrate this:

- All counties, whatever their size, returned two MPs to Parliament. Rutland was the smallest, with a population of just 19,000. Yet the industrialised county of Lancashire, with a population of 1,300,000, had only two seats.
- The differences were even more marked in the boroughs. In Cornwall, where medieval kings had granted borough status to many ports and fishing villages, there were 21 borough seats, sending 42 MPs to Parliament, although the population of Cornwall was only 192,000. Yet the city of Manchester, with a population of 180,000 in 1831, had no seat of its own. That did not mean that none of those living in Manchester could vote: those who owned property worth 40 shillings (£2) could vote in the county election for Lancashire but they had to travel all the way from Manchester to the county town of Lancaster, a journey of several hours, to cast their vote. Like Manchester, the fast-growing cities of Birmingham (population 144,000) and Leeds (population 123,000) had no seat of their own in Parliament.
- The south of England was hugely over-represented. Forty per cent of the seats in Parliament belonged to counties and boroughs that were situated south of a line from Bristol to London. The rural south was disproportionately over-represented in Parliament at the expense of the new industrial heartlands of the North, Scotland and the Midlands.

The reform campaign after 1815

Key question
Why did the middle classes oppose 'one man, one vote'?

After 1815, some of the loudest calls for reform came from the working classes and soon there developed a radical campaign calling for complete **manhood suffrage**. (This campaign is examined in Chapter 2, pages 18–27.)

However, most of the property-owning middle classes did not support this radical campaign. They were just as opposed to demands for complete manhood suffrage as the landowning classes. They did not want democracy where all men had the vote. That would be 'mob rule'. Instead, they wanted the vote for men like themselves, 'responsible' citizens who owned property.

Key term

Manhood suffrage
The right to vote for all adult men.

There was a widespread belief among the middle and upper classes that only those who owned property had a right to vote. They believed that only those who had a stake in the country, in the form of property, could be entrusted with the vote. For this reason most of the property-owning classes, whether rural or urban, opposed the radical reform campaign in the years from 1815 to 1820.

The demand for reform in the 1820s

When the economy revived in the early 1820s the demand for reform became quieter. In 1820, the Whig leader, Earl Grey, told his son-in-law that he did not expect to see a Reform Act 'during my life, or even yours'. Some of the Whigs put forward reform proposals for **disenfranchising** small boroughs and transferring their seats to larger towns and counties but these never secured enough support in the House of Commons. From 1824 to 1829 there were no petitions for reform presented to Parliament.

However, the demand for some kind of reform never subsided completely. The reformers continued to highlight the worst abuses of the unreformed system so that rotten boroughs such as Dunwich and Old Sarum became notorious. In 1821 Parliament even agreed to disenfranchise the corrupt Cornish borough of Grampound and allot its two seats to Yorkshire. In the more stable political climate of the 1820s parliamentary reform seemed a respectable and realistic goal for the middle classes. The problem was that, while the Tories dominated government, there was little chance of reform being passed by Parliament.

Then, in the late 1820s, the Tory Party and government began to fall apart (see pages 40–5) and the demand for reform began to gather more support. The fundamental reason was still the widespread belief that more people should have a say in government and that Parliament should not be controlled just by wealthy landowners, especially now that industry and commerce were so much more important in the British economy and society. This re-emerging demand for reform occurred at a time of growing economic discontent (1829–31) and was shown in the revival or establishment of political unions (see page 47) across the country. In the six months from October 1830 to April 1831, over 3000 petitions calling for reform were handed to Parliament. It was in these circumstances that the Whigs came to power and introduced proposals for the reform of Parliament.

Key question
Why was there a growing demand for reform in the late 1820s?

Disenfranchising
Taking away the right to a seat in Parliament.

Key term

Summary diagram: Support for reform

Growing demand for parliamentary reform
to give more seats in Parliament to new, industrial towns and cities

Middle classes wanted more say in government
with votes for all property owners

More radical, working-class demand is for universal manhood suffrage
so that all men have the vote

Reform movement gathers pace in late 1820s
with growth of political unions

Key question
Why did the Whigs introduce a Reform Bill in 1831?

3 | The Reform Bill in the House of Commons 1830–1

As recently as 1827, Earl Grey had shown very little interest in parliamentary reform. There did not seem to be huge public support and the king was certainly opposed to it. But over the next three years the whole political scene changed dramatically. This transformation was caused by:

- the disintegration of the Tory Party
- the passing of Catholic Emancipation
- the accession to the throne of King William IV
- the revival of interest in reform.

These developments are all discussed fully in Chapter 3.

Key date
Whig government was appointed: November 1830

By 1830, the Whigs could see that parliamentary reform might be a vote-winner and, in the 1830 general election, many opponents of reform were defeated. Although the Whigs still did not have a majority in Parliament, many of them felt that support for reform might be their best way to get back to power after over 30 years in opposition.

The Whig government, which was appointed in November 1830, decided to make parliamentary reform a priority, especially as there was mounting agitation in the country. But it was not easy to agree on the contents of such reform. Clearly, the government would have to deal with the worst abuses of the present system. That would mean getting rid of the rotten boroughs and providing seats in Parliament for the big new towns that were not boroughs. But Earl Grey and his ministers were not revolutionaries. They wished to preserve rule by the landed classes, men like themselves, with the support of the middle classes, and to 'purify' the present system. In order to work out the details of the reform, Grey formed a four-man committee and instructed them to produce reform proposals that were:

- 'large enough to satisfy public opinion and to afford sure ground for resistance to further innovation'
- 'yet so based on property, and on existing franchises and territorial divisions, as to run no risk of overthrowing the [existing] form of government'.

Let us examine these instructions more closely. Grey wanted reform:

- *Large enough to satisfy public opinion*: enough to pacify the demands coming from meetings, petitions, demonstrations and the press.
- *To afford sure ground for resistance to further innovation*: reform which would settle the agitation once and for all.
- *Based on property*: voting qualifications based on property, certainly not **universal suffrage**. Grey did not want democracy.
- *Existing franchises and territorial divisions*: Grey was probably thinking of the 40 shilling (£2) qualification in the counties and wanted to preserve constituency boundaries.

Key term
Universal suffrage
The vote for all people. In practice, at this time, it meant for all men, i.e. manhood suffrage.

- *Run no risk of overthrowing the [existing] form of government*: Grey believed in aristocratic government and wanted to win over the middle classes and bring them into partnership with the landowners. He wanted to 'reform in order to preserve'.

Profile: Earl Grey 1764–1845

1764	–	Born Charles Grey into an aristocratic Whig family in Northumberland
1786	–	Elected MP for Northumberland
1793 and 1797	–	Introduced bills for parliamentary reform which were defeated
1806	–	Became leader of the Whigs in the Commons
1807	–	Inherited his father's title of Earl and moved to the House of Lords
1830–4	–	Prime Minister of Whig government
1845	–	Died

From his early days in Parliament, Grey had been a supporter of moderate parliamentary reform as the best way to get rid of the injustices of the old system and avoid revolution. He was leader of the Whigs through the years of Lord Liverpool and Tory domination and did not come to power until Wellington's Tory government collapsed in 1830. Grey is mainly remembered for steering the Reform Bill through Parliament in 1831–2.

The first Reform Bill, March 1831

The reform committee made proposals to the full Cabinet and a **bill** was presented to the House of Commons in March 1831. It produced an 'absolutely electrifying shock'. Most MPs had expected a fairly moderate measure, getting rid of some rotten boroughs and transferring their seats to a few of the bigger towns. Instead, the Bill:

- deprived 60 boroughs with populations of under 2000 of both of their MPs
- deprived 47 boroughs of between 2000 and 4000 people of one of their MPs
- awarded seats in Parliament to 11 large towns which were to gain two MPs each
- awarded seats in Parliament to 21 towns to gain one MP each
- established a uniform voting qualification in the boroughs: all those who owned or rented a house worth £10 a year in rent
- confirmed the existing voting qualification in the counties to be ownership of property worth 40 shillings (£2) a year
- awarded some counties, such as Yorkshire, more seats.

Key date

First Reform Bill introduced to Parliament: March 1831

Key term

Bill
A proposal for reform put forward in Parliament.

The Whig minister Lord John Russell introduces the Reform Bill in the House of Lords.

Opposition to the Reform Bill

Key question
What arguments were
made by opponents
of reform?

The Tories were horrified at the reform proposals. Sir Robert
Peel, the Tory leader in the Commons, opposed the Bill because:

- it disenfranchised small boroughs which had been represented
  by great men like William Pitt and George Canning
- it would change existing voting qualifications which, because
  they varied from borough to borough, made sure that different
  interests were represented in different types of borough
- it would not be 'final' because further demands for reform
  would later be made. MPs would see that they could gain
  popularity by promising further change and so, in Peel's words,
  they 'will offer votes and power to a million men and will quote
  your precedent [example]'.

In response to Peel and other Tories, a young Whig, Thomas
Macaulay, stressed that most of the working classes would not
qualify under the £10 householder qualification in the boroughs.
Rather, he said, the Bill would enfranchise those with 'property
and intelligence', the middle classes. They would be won over 'to
the side of security and stability' and thus provide the best
possible guarantee against a revolution.

In fact, most MPs, whether Whig or Tory, wanted to maintain
stability and avoid a revolution. The difference was that Tories
like Peel thought that giving in to demands for reform would
endanger the whole political system and bring revolution nearer,
whereas the Whigs thought that reform would stave off revolution
by winning over the middle classes and stifling the demand for
complete manhood suffrage.

Reformers chopping down a tree of rotten boroughs while opposition Tories try to prop it up. Ordinary British people watch from a distance as the sun rises.

There were a small number of more radical MPs in Parliament. Most of them supported the Bill, often regarding it as a 'first instalment' of reform, but Henry Hunt was convinced that the Whig policy:

> was to get one million of the middle classes, the little shopkeepers and those people, to join the higher classes … and thus unite together to keep their hands still in the pockets of the seven millions.

(a) Who are the 'seven millions'?
(b) Why should the middle and higher classes wish to 'keep their hands still in the pockets of the seven millions'?

The defeat of the Bill, April 1831

When the vote was taken on the second reading of the Bill in the House of Commons the government won by a single vote. However, when the Bill was examined in detail in committee (see the box on page 65), it was picked apart and it became clear that major amendments would be made. The Whigs were furious. They were determined to have their Bill and knew that there was huge support for it in the country. They asked King William IV to dissolve Parliament and call a new election. If they secured a large majority in Parliament, they would inflict a defeat on the Tories. Furthermore, once reform had enfranchised the middle classes, the Whigs were confident of being able to stay in power for many years. The king, however, was reluctant to agree. After all, there had been a general election just six months before. And, with recent poor harvests, 'Swing' riots in the countryside (see pages 46–7) and huge political demonstrations in the cities, the atmosphere was already over-heated.

Grey, however, was determined. He persuaded the king that reform of Parliament would pacify public opinion and cause the agitation in the country to die down. In other words, reform would be the best guarantee of peace and stability. First, however, the Whigs had to secure a majority in Parliament in order to get reform passed. With these arguments, Grey persuaded the king to call an election.

The stages by which a bill becomes an Act of Parliament

First reading: an announcement to the House of Commons that a proposal for reform will be introduced.

Second reading: the main outlines of the bill are debated and voted on. If defeated in a vote, the proposal is withdrawn.

Committee stage: a committee of MPs study the bill in detail and can make amendments.

Report stage: the bill is reported back to the full House of Commons where it can be debated and amended.

Third reading: the amended bill is 'read' and passed.

In the House of Lords, the bill goes through the same procedure as in the Commons. The Lords can reject a bill passed by the Commons (this was true up to 1911).

Royal assent: when the bill has passed through both Houses of Parliament, the monarch signs it and it becomes law, an Act of Parliament. The monarch has not refused to sign a bill since 1703.

'The Bill, the whole Bill and nothing but the Bill!'

Right across the country, there was huge backing for 'The Bill, the whole Bill and nothing but the Bill!' Although it would not give the vote to most of the working classes, the Bill still attracted widespread support. After all, this was the first major reform of Parliament for 200 years and, even if manhood suffrage was not granted immediately, many radicals thought it was more likely to be passed later by a reformed Parliament.

Most of the middle-class reformers did not want manhood suffrage. But they knew that they needed the support of huge numbers behind their demand for reform in order to convince the government not to back down. This national agitation enabled the government to keep up the pressure on the king and those in Parliament who were opposed to reform.

The election campaign was characterised by vast open-air meetings, with banners waving and music blaring. Major newspapers, such as *The Times*, supported reform and gave huge coverage to meetings and petitions for reform. The leaders of the reform movement emphasised that reform would be good for 'The Nation' and for 'The People'. In this way, they papered over any divisions between what the moderates and the more radical reformers wanted. This appearance of class unity was quite new and created the impression of a relentless, unanimous movement for reform.

The second Reform Bill, June–September 1831

The election swept the Whigs back to power with a majority of over 130 seats in Parliament. In 76 of the 82 county seats, where voting was generally freer than in the boroughs, pro-reform candidates were successful. Many aristocratic patrons found that, despite their money and their influence, their candidates were defeated.

The Whigs introduced a second Reform Bill. It was slightly more moderate than the first: the main change was that the Whigs agreed to a Tory amendment that extended the vote in the counties to tenants who rented land worth £50 a year, not just to those owning property worth £2 a year. This was a concession to the landed classes as it was expected that these tenant farmers would vote the same way as their landlords. This might placate some of the landowning Tories, while many of the Whigs, themselves mostly landowners, were happy to support this conservative move. After all, the Whigs intended that this reform should preserve a Britain dominated by the landowning classes.

The second Reform Bill was eventually passed by a majority of more than 100 votes in September 1831. Now it would have to be passed by the House of Lords. This is where it could easily be rejected as the Tories were in a large majority in the upper house. In early October, before the Bill was presented to the Lords, Thomas Attwood, the leader of the **Birmingham Political Union** (BPU), had a meeting with Grey. Attwood was planning a big demonstration and Grey hinted that now was the time for the BPU to make itself felt.

Attwood organised a huge march in Birmingham. It was to be orderly, to impress the authorities, and a reporter from *The Times* was invited to ensure publicity. About 100,000 joined in, ranging from bankers to miners. Speeches were made and a petition for Parliament was approved. The next day, Attwood presented the petition, along with 79 others from around the country, to Parliament. *The Times* reported the march of the previous day and warned the aristocracy not to resist the people. Would the Lords take note of the warning?

Key question
How was the second Reform Bill passed?

Key dates

General election: May 1831

Second Reform Bill introduced: June 1831

Key term

Birmingham Political Union
Formed in 1830 by Thomas Attwood, a banker from Birmingham, in order to campaign for Parliamentary reform. It attracted middle- and working-class support although Attwood did not believe in universal suffrage, but wanted the vote to be given to the middle classes who would then represent the views of the workers.

Summary diagram: The Reform Bill 1830–1

Introduction of Reform Bill, March 1831

Whig view of reform
It would preserve existing system
It would prevent revolution
It would be 'final'

Tory view of reform
It would be 'destructive'
It would incite revolution
It would lead to more radical change

Defeat of Bill and general election, April–May 1831

↓

Massive support for reform in the country and Whigs win election

↓

Second Bill passes Commons and is sent to House of Lords

Key question
How and why did Grey warn the Lords of the dangers of rejecting reform?

4 | The King, the Lords and the Country 1831–2

When the Bill was introduced to the House of Lords, the Prime Minister, Earl Grey, warned his fellow peers of what would happen if they rejected the Bill:

> Will your Lordships reject a measure sanctioned [agreed] by an overwhelming majority of representatives of the people in the other House – the people themselves, at the same time, roused and agitated from one end of the country to the other. I implore your Lordships to consider what will be the consequences of the rejection of this measure; and whether, if rejected now, it can finally be put aside. May you, my Lords, be wise in time and avoid those dangers which will inevitably arise from your rejection of this measure, and secure, by its adoption, peace and conciliation in the country.

Key date
The House of Lords rejected the second Reform Bill: October 1831

Rejection and riots, October 1831

In October 1831 the House of Lords rejected the second Reform Bill: 158 voted for, 199 against. In London, one commentator noted that the shops stayed shut, fearing riots and looting. Placards went up. One simply said: '199 against 22,000,000', referring to the number of peers who had voted against the bill compared to the population of Britain as a whole. The leaders of the political unions stepped up their pressure on the Whig government so that the Whig leaders would not lose their nerve and back down.

In the country as a whole, there was great anger. Riots broke out in several cities. In Nottingham, the castle, owned by the Duke of Newcastle, a leading opponent of reform, was burnt down. In Derby, the jail was destroyed. But the worst violence erupted in Bristol. It started on 29 October and crowds went on the rampage for three days. One of the main targets was the Bishop, who had voted against the Bill in the Lords: his palace was burnt down. So was the house of the Bristol MP, Charles Wetheral, an outspoken opponent of reform. Many government buildings were also destroyed. The city centre was ruined and looting was widespread. Events in Bristol alarmed both government and opposition, upper and middle classes.

The government response to the riots

The ruling classes, Whig and Tory, were alarmed by such a breakdown of law and order. It showed how spontaneous, unorganised action could spiral out of control. Their response was ruthless. In Bristol, a cavalry charge led to 12 deaths and many more injuries, either by the sword or by being driven back into burning buildings. Later, several of the rioters were hanged. The Whig government proved that it could be just as tough as it had been when dealing with law-breakers during the Swing riots (see pages 46–7).

The middle classes were just as shocked at this show of force by the masses. It was the kind of action that would bring discredit to the reform movement. Above all, it might scare the government into backing down and dropping their reform proposals. It would certainly strengthen the Tories' accusation that reform would lead to revolution and civil war. For the reformers, both inside and outside Parliament, it was essential to show that the reform movement was organised and disciplined, responsible and law-abiding. If that was the case, then the government would have no pretext for suppressing meetings and demonstrations and the Tory opposition would have no reason for blaming the reformers for the disorder.

The response of the political unions

The middle-class leaders of the political unions, men like Thomas Attwood of the BPU, understood this well. They needed the support of the masses in order to keep up a sustained pressure on the Whig government. But they also had to avoid giving the government any reason for repression. A well-coordinated, national reform movement would be far harder to defeat than a violent mob.

Attwood and other leaders of the campaign outside Parliament now found themselves caught between the Tory opponents of reform and the masses. The latter threatened to discredit the moderate reformers and they might scare the Whig government into losing its nerve. The reformers wanted peaceful, mass protest, both as a warning to the Tories and to strengthen the government's resolve.

Meanwhile, however, more militant members of the political unions were demanding more active, forceful agitation. Some of the more radical leaders were pointing out that the Whig Reform Bill was deliberately designed to exclude the working classes. Henry Hunt, one of the few radical MPs in Parliament, said that

Key question
What effect did the riots of autumn 1831 have on the government and its supporters?

'the bill will exclude nine-tenths of the male adult population from any share in the representation whatever'. The Whigs, and their allies outside, had to take the initiative if their moderate Reform Bill was to be passed.

Key question
Why did the Whigs need the support of the king?

Key dates

The Whig government introduced third Reform Bill: December 1831

The House of Lords rejected the Bill and the Whigs resigned: 7 May 1832

The king and the Lords 1831–2

In December 1831 the Whigs introduced a third Reform Bill and it passed the Commons with a 2:1 majority. Now the question was: would the Lords reject yet another Reform Bill? If so, what action would the government take? And, what was the attitude of the king?

The king, under pressure from Earl Grey, said that he would consider creating enough Whig peers to enable the Bill to pass the Lords. The Cabinet estimated that this might mean creating 50 or 60 peers. But for how *long* would the king agree to this? After all, many members of Parliament felt that such a request from the government would be putting too much pressure on the king. Even Lord Melbourne, the Home Secretary, thought it 'a much more violent and permanent measure in its effects' than asking the king to dissolve Parliament again. And Grey himself thought that to create as many as 50 or 60 peers was 'a measure of extreme force'. Furthermore, it would set a precedent for a future Tory government that could pack the House of Lords with Tories and block legislation passed by the elected House of Commons. The Whig leaders called for patience. But many reformers, both in Parliament and in the country as a whole, feared that the Whig leaders were weakening.

In April 1832, Grey introduced the Bill in the House of Lords. He spoke of the 'clamour outside', referring to the agitation across Britain, of 'a great and intelligent people' who deserved to have some say in the government of the country. The debate lasted for five days. Some of the speeches lasted for two or three hours. Finally, at dawn on 15 April, after a debate that went on through the night by candlelight, the Lords passed the new Bill. But it still had to be examined by a House of Lords' committee and this is where it could be unpicked and sent back, as an amended Bill, to the Commons. The political temperature was rising.

The Whig government resigns, May 1831

The pressure was also building up outside Parliament. At a huge meeting of the BPU on 7 May (see picture overleaf), Attwood made his most famous statement: 'I would rather die than see the great Bill of Reform rejected or mutilated in any of its great parts or provisions'. Grey and the Whig leaders now told the king that if the bill was not passed unamended, they would resign. This may have been intended as a threat; reports from the Court suggested that the king's advisers were opposed to the creation of more peers. The Whig leaders may have been bluffing. If so, their bluff was called: when the Lords' committee rejected the Bill on 7 May, the Whigs were forced to resign. The king now looked to the Tories to form a government. It was widely expected that the Duke of Wellington would lead a new government.

The meeting of the Birmingham Political Union on 7 May 1832.

The 'Days of May' 1832

Although the Whig leaders may have been surprised at how quickly the king accepted their resignations, some of them seemed quite relieved. Months of tension, pressure and argument had taken their toll. Perhaps the whole reform question could be settled by a Tory government with the support of moderate Whigs in Parliament. The Whigs had now lost the initiative and were on the back foot. They could only wait and see: Would the Duke be able to form a government? What would be the reaction of the political unions?

The Duke of Wellington, who had accused the Whigs of inciting revolution with their Reform Bill in April, now recognised that any new government would have to pass some kind of parliamentary reform in order to settle the whole question and calm the widespread agitation. Several of the Ultra Tories (see page 42) refused to serve in a government that was going to pass reform. Some of them were still angry with Wellington and Peel for pushing through Catholic Emancipation. The key question was: what would Peel's reaction be? It would be difficult to form any Tory government without the active support and leadership of Sir Robert Peel in the Commons. Peel was not completely opposed to reform. In fact, he realised the whole question needed to be settled. But, he was not going to be the one to do it. He had opposed the first Reform Bill and he refused to go back on his word. Peel had been accused of breaking his word over Catholic Emancipation and he was not going to damage his career even further by doing so again.

Key question
What difficulties did Wellington have in forming a government?

Key question
How effective was the threat of mass resistance?

'To stop the Duke, Go for Gold'

While Wellington tried to form a government the political unions were determined to do all they could to block any Tory administration. They believed a Tory reform would be much weaker. Above all, they feared that a Tory government would use military force to ban their meetings and break up their demonstrations. There was talk of mass refusal to pay taxes and even of armed resistance. On 12 May a meeting of delegates from various political unions met in London. During the meeting, **Francis Place** printed on a piece of paper:

Francis Place
A tailor by trade who had been active in radical politics since the 1790s. He had been largely responsible for the repeal of the Combination Acts in 1824 (see page 39). Previously a supporter of manhood suffrage, Place now accepted the need to work with men of 'money and influence' in order to get the Reform Bill passed.

Rough-sharpening
Sharpening swords in such a way that they would inflict 'a ragged wound', one more likely to fester and cause slow death.

TO STOP THE
DUKE
GO FOR
GOLD

Place was proposing that those holding paper money should demand its gold equivalent from the banks, thus depleting stocks and causing a financial collapse. This would cause massive disruption to the economy so that businesses would not be able to borrow money to keep up their production. Place believed that 'the bulk of the people would rise, en masse, at the call of the unions.' This was the kind of widespread, but peaceful, resistance that a government would find difficult to handle. Within four hours of the meeting, placards with Place's newly coined slogan were appearing all over London and being distributed to other towns.

The threat of civil war

Wellington hated the political unions: he could not see the difference between the more militant unions and the constitutional, non-violent ones. As far as he was concerned, they were all as bad as each other; they were creating disorder and were planning an armed uprising. Therefore, they should be put down with force. In October 1831 he had said: 'The people of England are very quiet if they are left alone; and if they won't [be quiet], there is a way to make them.'

Would the Duke carry out this threat? A soldier, Alexander Somerville, wrote in his diary: 'It was rumoured that the Birmingham Political Union was to march for London that night and that we were to stop it on the road.' On Sunday 13 May his regiment was ordered to start '**rough-sharpening**' their swords. This was the first time the soldiers had been ordered to do this since the Battle of Waterloo in 1815.

The air was full of rumour, gossip and bluff. Some of the unions were said to be carrying out military drills and talking of armed resistance. Would Wellington be able to rely on the loyalty of the troops or would they refuse to use their swords against civilians? Place's call for a 'run on the banks' was effective. The banks' stocks of gold, which had been falling for some time, were now falling even more quickly and the leading banker, Lord Rothschild, warned that only the recall of Earl Grey would stop the slide. Such was the overheated, tense atmosphere of the so-called 'Days of May' in 1832.

Key date
Wellington failed to form a Tory government and the Whigs returned to power: 14 May 1832

'Up and Down', a cartoon published on 18 May 1832. John Bull, who represents the ordinary man, puts his weight under Earl Grey's end of the political seesaw in order to push Wellington down. The king is in the middle. How accurately does this cartoon portray the ending of the crisis of May 1832?

The king recalls the Whigs, May 1832

On 14 May Wellington had to face the fact that he could not form a government; too many leading Tories were refusing to serve in his Cabinet. Ultimately, it was Wellington's inability to form a government that led to the end of the crisis. When he admitted that he could not form a government, the king had no choice but to ask the Whigs to return. This time, they insisted on a firm promise. They would only return once the king had promised to appoint the necessary number of Whig peers to get the Reform Bill passed by the Lords. He agreed but, in the event, he did not need to carry out this promise. The king's secretary let it be known that he wanted the Lords to drop their opposition. Most of them did so and abstained from voting. The Bill was finally passed in early June.

Key question
Why did the king recall the Whig government?

The Lords finally passed the Reform Bill: June 1832

Key date

Summary diagram: The king, the Lords and the country 1831–2

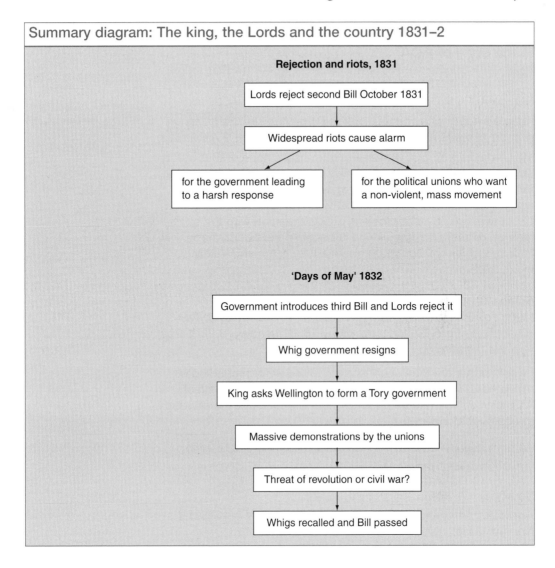

Rejection and riots, 1831

Lords reject second Bill October 1831

↓

Widespread riots cause alarm

for the government leading to a harsh response

for the political unions who want a non-violent, mass movement

'Days of May' 1832

Government introduces third Bill and Lords reject it

↓

Whig government resigns

↓

King asks Wellington to form a Tory government

↓

Massive demonstrations by the unions

↓

Threat of revolution or civil war?

↓

Whigs recalled and Bill passed

Study Guide: AS Questions

In the style of AQA

Read the following sources and answer the questions that follow.

Source A

Adapted from: speech made by the Prime Minister, Earl Grey, in support of the Reform Bill, in the House of Lords, on 9 April 1832.

My Lords, I admit that we have of late, heard none of that outcry on the part of the people which first marked the progress of this Bill. In its place a fearful silence at present prevails – a silence which may perhaps lead some persons foolishly to imagine that the people are no longer looking at this question with the same feelings of interest. That silence is because the people hope that your Lordships will no longer oppose their often and loudly expressed wishes.

Source B

From: speech made by Thomas Attwood, at a meeting of the Birmingham Political Union on 7 May 1832, just before the Lords rejected the third Bill.

I would rather die than see the great Bill of Reform rejected or mutilated … I see that you are all of one mind on the subject. Answer me then, had you not all rather die than live the slaves of the boroughmongers*?

[*A term used to describe rich people, often aristocrats, who controlled parliamentary boroughs.]

Source C

Adapted from: Aristocracy and People, Britain 1815–1865, by Norman Gash, 1979.

The House of Lords had to be threatened with a mass creation of peers before it gave way. The King had to undergo the humiliating experience of taking the Whigs back after he had dismissed them because Wellington could not provide him with an alternative government.

(a) **Use Source A and your own knowledge**
   Explain briefly what is meant by 'that outcry on the part of the people which first marked the progress of this Bill.'   (3 marks)

(b) **Use Source B and your own knowledge**
   Explain how useful Source B is as evidence of the threat posed by the Birmingham Political Union in May 1832.   (7 marks)

(c) **Use Sources A, B and C and your own knowledge**
   'It was Wellington's inability to form a government, rather than the threat of revolution, that led to the passing of the Reform Act in June 1832.' Explain why you agree or disagree with this statement.   (15 marks)

Exam tips

The cross-references are intended to take you straight to the material that will help you to answer the questions.

(a) In question **(a)** you should provide a brief explanation of the popular outcry in the context of:

- the meetings and demonstrations in support of the Bill
- in particular, you should refer to the riots which followed the Lords' rejection of the Bill in October 1831 (page 67).

(b) In question **(b)** you have to evaluate the usefulness of the source, showing that you understand:

- who Attwood and the Birmingham Political Union were
- the specific threat, if any, which they posed in May 1832 to the government, to the Lords.

    You should then explain whether you think this speech was:

- a threat of armed uprising
- or a warning to the Lords of the consequences if they rejected the Bill
- or was it just rhetoric, stirring words to keep up the spirits of his listeners (or of the Whig government) (pages 66–71)?

(c) In question **(c)** you need to examine the reasons for the passing of the Reform Act, weighing up the importance of Wellington's failure to form a government against other factors. In doing so, you should make full use of the sources:

- Does source A suggest that popular pressure was an important factor? Would the Lords have interpreted references to 'outcry' and 'fearful silence' as a warning of revolutionary threat? It did not stop them from rejecting the Bill!
- Does Source B represent a genuine threat of rebellion? Or just an attempt to influence the Lords vote or strengthen the government's nerve?
- The author of Source C is a historian, not a participant in the events (so can his words be taken at face value?). He stresses the parliamentary crisis, Wellington's inability to form a government and the king's role rather than revolutionary threat.

    In conclusion, you need to bring in other factors such as the widespread recognition that there had to be *some* reform in order to quell the agitation in the country (pages 61–72). Then you should arrive at a balanced conclusion.

In the style of Edexcel

Answer both parts of the question below.

(a) What pressure did the political unions exert on
government and Parliament in order to get the Reform Bill
passed?   (20 marks)
(b) How serious was the threat of revolution during the Reform
crisis of 1830–2?   (40 marks)

Exam tips

*The cross-references are intended to take you straight to the material
that will help you to answer the questions.*

(a) In question (a) you should use your own knowledge in order to
explain:

- what the unions were, and identify significant leaders
- the way they pressurised the Whig government and
  threatened the Tories (especially in the Lords)
- the importance of mass support and direct action while
  remaining peaceful
- the significance of national agitation in getting the Bill passed
  (pages 66–72).

(b) This question carries twice as many marks so you need to write
a mini-essay. You should:
- identify the nature of the threat posed by the unions, e.g. (i) at
  a time of Swing riots and mass unemployment (1830–1) and
  (ii) in organised mass meetings and the 'run on the banks' in
  1831–2
- explain how much of a genuine threat was posed by talk of
  refusal to pay taxes and armed resistance
- explain whether a greater threat of revolution was posed by
  those outside the unions, e.g. as in the riots of October 1831.
  How great was the threat of that happening again, and on a
  larger scale, in 1832?

A successful revolution leads to the overthrow of a government, or a
system of government. How close was that in 1830–2? Would the
unions and their supporters have resisted a Tory government led by
the Duke of Wellington? If so, was there any danger of the
government not being able to rely on its troops? At the end, you will
need to draw together the main strands of your argument and make
an overall judgement about how serious the threat of revolution was
(pages 61–72).

What was the Importance of the Reform Act?

POINTS TO CONSIDER
The key historical debate has focused on the question of how much changed and how much stayed the same as a result of the Reform Act. The key terms of the Act, and the elements of change and continuity, are examined in this chapter under the following headings:

- The effects of the Reform Act
- The importance of the Reform Act

1 | The Effects of the Reform Act

> **Key question**
> How much was changed by the Reform Act and how much stayed the same?

The main terms of the Act are summarised in the box below.

The redistribution of seats
- 56 rotten and pocket boroughs lost both of their MPs
- 30 boroughs lost one MP
- 22 new boroughs with two MPs were created and 14 of these were in London and the northern industrial towns – Manchester, Leeds, Bradford, Sheffield, Bolton, Blackburn, etc.
- 19 new boroughs with one MP were created
- 64 new county seats were created so that the more populous counties gained more seats
- 18 English seats were transferred to Scotland, Wales and Ireland.

Voting qualifications
In the boroughs
- Adult males owning or occupying property worth £10 a year in rent.

In the counties
- Adult males owning property worth £2 a year
- Adult males renting land worth £50 a year.

Change and continuity in the Reform Act

The main elements of change and continuity are summarised in the box on the next page.

Change and continuity in the 1832 Reform Act

Elements of change	Elements of continuity
Redistribution of seats	
A total of 145 borough seats were abolished. This was a massive change, especially as there had been virtually no changes for hundreds of years.	About 70 pocket boroughs remained, mostly in the control of prominent landowners.
Many of these seats were awarded to the large towns and cities of the north and other industrial areas. As a result, there was a huge increase in the number of urban voters.	31 boroughs had less than 300 voters while cities like Manchester, Leeds and Birmingham each had several thousands so there were still huge differences in the size of electorates.
The number of county seats was increased and, generally, these were more 'open' seats, less likely to be controlled by individual patrons or prominent landowners.	The rural south was still over-represented relative to the industrial north, as were small country towns relative to bigger industrial towns, some of which still did not gain parliamentary seats.
Electorate/voting qualifications	
There was now a uniform system of franchises or, rather, two systems: one for borough, and one for county, constituencies. This replaced the confusing variety of franchises under the old system.	Ownership of property was still the basis of the franchise. This meant that the vast majority of the working classes were excluded from the electoral system.
It is difficult to assess the increase in size of the electorate because we do not have accurate figures for the number of voters before 1832 but historians estimate that the electorate increased from about 490,000 to 800,000 which is a rise of about 65 per cent. Nearly one in five adult males now had the vote in England; fewer in Scotland, Wales and Ireland.	Less than 20 per cent of adult males could vote in England. An even smaller percentage was able to vote in Scotland, Wales and Ireland.
In Scotland, where there had been a very restricted electorate, the number of voters increased from 4500 to 65,000.	Most of the working class were excluded from the vote. However, there were regional variations depending on house prices: the £10 householder qualification in the boroughs meant that some of the working class had the vote in London, but very few did in Leeds where house prices and rents were lower.
The biggest single occupational group to be enfranchised was shopkeepers. Most of the middle classes, and some skilled craftsmen, now had the vote.	Most of the new electors were small property owners, more interested in preserving their own property and privileges than in demanding further reforms, and so tended to be 'conservative'.
Power of the aristocracy	
The number of parliamentary seats controlled by members of the House of Lords was reduced as there were now far fewer pocket boroughs.	Landlords, many of them aristocratic, continued to exert influence, both in the remaining pocket boroughs and in county elections. The £50 tenant farmers enfranchised in the counties could be expected to vote the same way as their landlords, especially as voting was still 'open' and not secret.
The power and prestige of the House of Lords no longer seemed so formidable as they had been forced to back down over the	

passing of the Act. This had shown that a government with a majority in the Commons and the backing of the electorate could force a monarch to persuade the Lords to accept laws to which they were opposed. The dominance of the Commons was confirmed and enhanced.

Power of the middle classes

The new middle classes, especially the manufacturing interest, were now more solidly represented in Parliament. Many thousands of urban dwellers in cities such as Manchester, Birmingham, Leeds and Bradford now had the vote for the first time.

The middle classes had been recognised and admitted into the political system. Following the Reform Act, the Whigs introduced new, similar, voting qualifications for local government in 1835 and many businessmen became actively involved in local politics and administration. Here they were able to deal with the issues that affected everyday life, such as public health and education (which were not dealt with by central government in those days).

The example of successful extra-parliamentary pressure, led by the middle classes, was to be followed by the largely middle-class Anti-Corn Law League after 1838 (see Chapter 8).

Elections

There was a significant increase in the number of contested elections after 1832. In the previous 30 years, on average about 30 per cent of parliamentary seats were contested at election time. In the next 30 years, the average was to be over 50 per cent. In other words, there was a big increase in the number of people who had a real choice at election time.

Registration of voters

The need to have the names of all voters on an electoral register gave a boost to party organisation. This is explained more fully later.

Most Cabinet ministers and all Prime Ministers, in the next 30 years, except Sir Robert Peel, were members of the aristocracy.

Very few industrialists entered Parliament as MPs. There were several reasons:

- they were too busy running their own businesses, whereas big landowners left their estates in the hands of agents
- there was no payment for MPs
- you had to own land worth £600 to be able to stand as a parliamentary candidate.

Professional men, such as lawyers and doctors, continued to form the majority of middle-class MPs.

The landed classes continued to dominate Parliament. In the post-reform election of December 1832, about 75 per cent of the MPs elected were landowners. Fewer than 100 were from industrial or commercial backgrounds.

The diarist Charles Grenville noted that the Reform Parliament 'turns out to be very much like every other Parliament'.

With no secret ballot and a continuation of 'open' voting, there continued to be much bribery and intimidation. Employers and, especially, landlords still had much influence.

Elections continued to be as noisy and chaotic as before, as shown by Charles Dickens' *Morning Chronicle* report during the 1835 election in Northampton: 'The noise and confusion here this morning – which is the first day of polling – is so great that my head is actually splitting. There are about 40 flags on either side, two tremendous bands and vehicles are constantly driving about and down the town, conveying voters to the Poll; and guzzling and howling and roaring in every house of Entertainment.'

The registration of voters

The Reform Act required that all those entitled to vote should have their names entered on an electoral register before they could cast their vote. This gave a huge spur to party organisation as local Whigs and Tories tried to ensure that all their supporters were registered. The local parties also challenged the claims of their opponents' supporters (e.g. 'Did they have the right property qualifications?'). In this way, the Reform Act contributed to the development of more modern, organised political parties.

One politician who clearly recognised the increased need to manage elections was Peel and this was a key to the recovery of Tory electoral fortunes. When he and his party were returned to power after the election of 1841, it was the first occasion on which a government (the Whigs) with a parliamentary majority was defeated in an election by an opposition party (the Tories).

The Reform Act and the working classes

The working classes had provided some of the strongest support for the Whig Reform Bill during its passage through Parliament. Huge numbers had marched and demonstrated and Grey had certainly used the threat of a mass movement to put pressure on the king and the Lords. Why had the workers been so keen to support a measure from which they were to gain so little?

Key question
Why had the workers been so keen to support a measure from which they were to gain so little?

- The boldness of the Whig bill had captivated most people. Even Henry Hunt was prepared to vote for the Bill on the grounds that the removal of so many rotten boroughs was worthwhile.
- The stubbornness of the Tory resistance, particularly in the Lords, had provided a target on which all those who wanted change could focus. It meant that popular attention was diverted away from the limitations of the Act. Finally, in May 1832, the threat of a Tory government led by Wellington had produced almost unanimous support for the Whig Bill.
- Some saw it as a 'first instalment' of reform. Although the Whig minister, Lord Russell, declared the Bill to be a 'final' act, some of the working classes believed that further reform (e.g. in working and living conditions) would follow.

Gradually, however, the truth sank in. The middle classes, once enfranchised, were satisfied, certainly not keen to see the propertyless masses gain the vote or even to support social reform. Once the excitement had died down, many of the working classes felt let down, even betrayed.

From the mid-1830s onwards, the working classes started to organise themselves again for further action. This was to show itself in the form of Chartism, the subject of Chapter 7.

2 | The Importance of the Reform Act

Many years after it was passed, the 1832 Act came to be known as the 'Great Reform Act'. It earned this title from Whig historians who looked back from the late nineteenth and early twentieth

Key question
How 'great' was the Great Reform Act?

centuries, after further parliamentary reform had been passed, and saw the Act paving the way towards the development of a fully democratic system of government. But that was to read history backwards. The last thing the Whigs wanted was democracy. If anything, Earl Grey and his ministers brought in reform to save the country from the 'evils' of democracy. So what did motivate the Whigs?

The Whig motives for reform

When Grey formed his Cabinet in 1830 he said that he wanted to show 'real capacity [ability] in the landed aristocracy' and he appointed one of the most aristocratic governments of the whole nineteenth century. Yet Grey's government introduced an unexpectedly bold reform bill. Why?

- *Party political gain*. The Whigs saw reform as a vote-winner and they would earn the gratitude of the newly enfranchised, especially the £10 householder in the boroughs. Furthermore, the majority of the pocket boroughs were in the hands of Tory, rather than Whig, landowners and it was the pocket boroughs that the Whigs targeted for abolition. However, there is little mention of this element of political gain in the diaries or letters of Whig ministers.
- *Fear of disorder and unrest, even revolution*. There was growing unrest in the country when the Whigs came to power. With riots in the countryside, poor harvests, rising unemployment, a depression in trade and the growth of political unions, there was widespread agitation. Reform might be one way to restore peace and stability. It would certainly be better to introduce reform from above than be swept away by revolution from below.
- *Enthusiasm for reform*. Some members of the Cabinet were ardent supporters of reform and had been so for a long time. Others, however, were more cautious. But most agreed that the parliamentary system needed 'purifying', with the removal of the worst and most blatant abuses. An obvious target was the rotten and pocket boroughs. Also, there had to be some recognition of the importance of industry and the demands of the new middle classes to be given some political power.

Key question
How significant an achievement was the passing of the Reform Act?

The Whig achievement

What made the need for reform so urgent was the growing sense of crisis. The Tory party was divided and their government had fallen apart. There was widespread agitation in the country at large and a growing expectation of reform. Furthermore, Catholic Emancipation (see page 42) had shown that a major constitutional reform could be carried out without endangering the State. The Whigs saw reform as the best way to restore peace and order, to stave off any threat of revolution, to keep themselves in power and to preserve the present system of government. All of these aims were achieved.

The Act may have been quite limited in its contents, but then it was not intended to lead to radical changes. Many aspects of the old system, some of them quite corrupt and unfair (certainly to us in the twenty-first century), were preserved but that was what the Whigs intended. The middle classes were taken into partnership with the landed classes and detached from their working-class allies. The middle classes did not take political power: they remained junior partners, as the Whigs had intended. The working classes stayed outside the political nation, again as intended. The Whigs achieved what they set out to do and they were well rewarded. In the first election after the Reform Act, they secured a majority of 308 in the House of Commons.

The Tories were right about some things. Sir Robert Peel had said the Act would not turn out to be 'final', as the Whig minister Lord Russell had said it would be. There was to be more parliamentary reform in 1867. But that was a generation away. Meanwhile, the Whigs had achieved the settlement of 'a great constitutional question', which they had set out to do.

The way the Act was passed was dramatic, involving a general election, stubborn resistance from the Lords, rioting, massive demonstrations, the threat of civil war and pressure on the king to force the Lords to give way. The details of the Bill were, perhaps, less important than the fact and the manner of its passing. As the MP John Bright said:

It was not a good Bill though it was a great Bill when it passed.

In the years to come, Britain avoided revolution. While the middle classes were leading revolutionary movements in Europe and succeeded in overthrowing governments in several countries (such as France), Britain avoided any such upheaval. In the middle years of the century, Britain became the most stable, the richest and the most powerful nation on earth. Much of the credit must go to the Whigs who passed the Reform Act.

Summary diagram: The importance of the Reform Act

Whig motives ⟶
- party political gain (over the Tories)
- fear of disorder or revolution
- enthusiasm for reform

The Whig achievement ⟶
- restored social and political order
- settled 'a great constitutional question'
- laid basis for future stability and prosperity

Study Guide: AS Questions

In the style of AQA

Study the following source material and then answer the questions that follow.

Source A

Adapted from: Poor Man's Guardian, *the radical journal with a wide working-class readership, commenting on the Reform Bill in September 1831.*

It is clear we GAIN nothing by it; but it is said that these middle men, whom this measure admits into a share of the law-making process, will be more inclined to hear our appeal for justice, and will return a majority favourable to it. Think it not. Why already – even before they have been admitted – do they not shut the doors of Parliament against you? For they will not tolerate our mention of Universal Suffrage.

Source B

Adapted from: letter written by Earl Grey to the king, November 1831.

The question of reform should be settled in the interests of the middle classes. If this could be done they would not only be separated from, but also placed in direct opposition to, those who threatened the safety of the country. Under such circumstances, the radicals would lose support. Furthermore, all those middle-class supporters of reform would become united with the government and seek to put down the radicals. The principle of reform is to prevent revolution.

Source C

Adapted from: Parliamentary Reform 1640–1832, John Cannon, 1973.

The theme of preservation and continuity runs through the whole bill, and if the outcome was to afford a new lease of life to aristocratic influence, it is scarcely a surprising result to issue from a government that was overwhelmingly aristocratic in composition.

(a) **Use Source A and your own knowledge**
Explain briefly the meaning of 'Universal Suffrage' in the context of the 1832 Reform Act. (3 marks)

(b) **Use Source B and your own knowledge**
How useful is this source as an explanation of Grey's attitude to reform? (7 marks)

(c) **Use Sources A, B and C and your own knowledge**
'Very little was changed by the 1832 Reform Act.' Explain why you agree or disagree with this view. (15 marks)

Exam tips

The cross-references are intended to take you straight to the material that will help you to answer the questions.

(a) In question **(a)** this meant the vote for all adult males, not considered for women at this time. Explain that universal suffrage would give the vote to the working classes which, in the view of the *Poor Man's Guardian*, is the last thing the middle classes want. Nor are the Whigs in favour. Do not write an essay – the question is only worth 3 marks.

(b) For question **(b)**, pages 61–2 will help here. Start by *explaining* Grey's attitude as shown in this source, e.g.

- to win over the middle classes so that they united with the government in resisting radical demands
- in this way, to prevent revolutionary change (such as introduction of universal suffrage).

    Then **evaluate** the source in order to judge how useful it is, e.g.

- what does it **not** tell us of Grey's attitude which might limit its usefulness – for instance, that Grey wanted middle-class support in order to prolong aristocratic domination of government
- how might his audience (i.e. the king) and the purpose of his writing (e.g. to persuade the king to put pressure on the Lords?) shape the views expressed – Grey is stressing revolutionary threat ('the safety of the country') in order to convince the king that the Whig bill will weaken that threat ('radicals would lose support').

    Conclude by making a judgement about how full or reliable an explanation this source provides.

(c) A mini-essay is demanded for question **(c)** as it has 15 marks. You will need a full knowledge of the terms of the Act (page 77) as well as an understanding of how much change was signified by those terms (so re-read the rest of this short chapter). You should start by explaining what the sources tell us of change and continuity. Your own, wider knowledge will undoubtedly inform your explanations.

- Source A refers to change ('middle men' gaining 'a share of the legislature') as well as continuity ('doors of Parliament shut against you') which you should explain, e.g. how much of a share did middle classes get in making the laws in Parliament?
- Source B – to what extent was reform being 'settled in the interests of the middle classes'? To what extent did it 'prevent revolution', if there was such a threat?
- Source C – show how 'the theme of preservation and continuity runs through the whole bill', if you think it does so, and how it gave 'a new lease of life to aristocratic influence'.

    A critical comment about the reliability, usefulness, etc., of the sources, while you are explaining what they tell us, would help to gain the top marks. Also you will need to show what the Act did *not* reform at all, e.g. open voting and bribery at elections, no payment for MPs. In conclusion, you will need to make judgements about the overall extent of change, especially those changes not touched on by the sources, for example:

- How much was the over-representation of the rural south, as opposed to the industrial north, redressed?
- What contribution did Reform make to the development of party organisation?
- Did Reform set a precedent, an example, for further reform?

In the style of Edexcel

Answer both parts of the question below.

(a) What were the motives of the Whigs in passing Reform in 1832? (20 marks)
(b) How much was the British political system changed by the 1832 Reform Act? (40 marks)

Exam tips

The cross-references are intended to take you straight to the material that will help you to answer the questions.

(a) Re-read pages 61–3 in Chapter 4 and page 81 in this chapter. In an exam, you should aim to complete question **(a)** in about 15–20 minutes, so no more than a side or 100–250 words of writing would be expected. Motives which you discuss are likely to include:

- Party political gain/keeping Whigs in power, e.g. winning the votes of the newly enfranchised, removing many Tory pocket boroughs.
- To purify existing system, getting rid of many pocket boroughs with tiny electorates and thus to preserve the essence of present system. There is evidence for this in the instructions Grey gave to the Committee that drafted the Bill (page 61) and in speeches by Whig leaders.
- To quell agitation and disorder already existing when Whigs came to power and which intensified during the passage of the Bill.
- To recognise the economic power and political aspirations of middle classes and bring them into partnership with aristocracy, thus isolating the more radical reformers and their working-class supporters.

In conclusion, you should decide which are the most important motives.

(b) Question **(b)** requires an essay, so it is worth spending 5 minutes planning it. One approach would be to take key aspects of the Act (e.g. redistribution of seats; voting qualifications; conduct of elections) and then note down whether the terms of the Act signify change or continuity in the political system as has been done in this chapter. As you deal with each aspect in the essay itself, you need to make judgements about *how much* was changed (and, of course, how much was not changed). If you do this, your essay will be analytical throughout. You will also need to examine change and continuity as shown in the composition and actions of the reformed Parliament. The actual terms of the Act will be of less importance here but issues to discuss include:

- the power and influence of the aristocracy versus the middle classes
- registration of voters and how this affected political life in the years to come.

If you are doing this question as revision and have already studied later Whig reforms of the 1830s, you might comment on what these show you about government and Parliament after the Reform Act. Also, you might comment on whether the Act was a final settlement or whether it set a precedent for further constitutional change. In conclusion, you should arrive at an overall judgement about how much was changed and back this up by two or three key pieces of supporting evidence.

6 The 1830s: A Decade of Reform

POINTS TO CONSIDER

The Whigs came under pressure to pass several more reforms following the 1832 Reform Act. These included reform of local government and the Church, as well as reform of living and working conditions for the poor. In this chapter these reforms are covered under the headings of:

- The pressures for reform
- The old Poor Law
- The Poor Law Amendment Act 1834
- Factory reform
- Reform of local government and the Church
- The decline of the Whigs and the 1841 election

Key dates

1795		Introduction of Speenhamland system
1830		Start of Ten Hours Movement
1832		Poor Law Commission set up
1833		Royal Commission into the Employment of Children in Factories
		Factory Act
		Reform of the Church of Ireland
1834		Poor Law Amendment Act
		Whigs forced to resign
	December	Peel became Prime Minister of a Tory/Conservative government
		Peel issued Tamworth Manifesto
1835	April	Peel resigned and Whigs returned to government
		Municipal Corporations Act
1836		Marriage Act allowed Nonconformists and Catholics to marry in their own churches
1837		Introduction of new Poor Law into the north of England
		King William died and was succeeded by Queen Victoria
1841		Conservatives won the general election
1842		Mines Act
1844		Factory Act
1847		Ten Hours Act

1 | The Pressures for Reform

The 1832 Reform Act was to be followed by several social reforms, as well as reform of local government, in the mid-1830s. The Whigs were fairly cautious, reforming in order to preserve, rather than trying to change society. But expectations of reform were raised by the 1832 Act. One minister told Earl Grey, the Prime Minister, that 'the Reform will lead to Revolution' unless further social reforms were passed. In fact, even before they had succeeded in passing the Reform Act, the government had set up a Commission to examine the way the State and local authorities dealt with the problem of poverty. Further reforms went on to deal with factory conditions, local government and the Church.

Not all of these reforms originated with the Whigs. Often they were the work of particular individuals or groups even if they required the support of the government in order to pass through Parliament. So where did the pressure for reform come from?

Before 1830, government had largely ignored increasing social problems, above all the problems brought on by industrialisation and the growth of cities. This was partly because issues like poverty, disease and factory conditions were not seen as the responsibility of central government. If they were government issues at all, it was local government that dealt with them. Yet, in the 1830s, a series of reforms was passed by the Whig government. Was this the work of a newly elected, reformed Parliament? Were the Whigs more willing to reform than the Tories had been? Were they more aware of social distress?

To understand further why and how reform was carried out in the 1830s, we need to look at some of the pressures for reform coming from outside Parliament.

Laissez-faire

Most people believed that the role of government should be limited to defence and foreign trade: all other matters should be dealt with locally. The views of **Adam Smith** were increasingly influential. In his book, *The Wealth of Nations*, he had argued that individuals should be free to follow their own best interests and the economy should be free of government control. Above all, government should not interfere in the relations between employer and employee. The latter should be left to work out rates of pay and hours of work without government interference. This theory of economic freedom was referred to as *laissez-faire*.

This *laissez-faire* view that individuals should be free to do what they wanted with their own property, including their money, was widely supported in the 1830s. Many property owners saw taxation as a form of confiscation of their property. The prevalence of *laissez-faire* views was one reason why there was to be so much resistance to reforms which extended government control and increased taxation.

But *laissez-faire* views did not go unchallenged. What if an individual, pursuing his own best interests, engaged in anti-social activities such as building slums or exploiting vulnerable people,

Key question
To what extent were the Whigs a reforming government?

Key question
What was the meaning of *laissez-faire*?

Key terms

Adam Smith
Scottish economist who argued that industry and trade flourished best when they were entirely free of government interference.

Laissez-faire
A French term, best translated as 'leave alone' or 'do not interfere'. The concept is associated with the free trade, economic ideas of Adam Smith.

like children working in factories? How could one balance individual freedom with government authority? One answer was provided by a lawyer and philosopher called Jeremy Bentham.

Jeremy Bentham and the theory of Utilitarianism

Bentham accepted the need for individual freedom and non-interference in the economy by the government, but he recognised that sometimes government interference was necessary. Not only was this interference necessary to defend people from attack and provide security, it was also needed to protect society against criminals. For the sake of the majority, the freedom of some individuals would need to be restricted. Bentham believed it was the government's job to promote 'the greatest happiness of the greatest number'.

In order to achieve this, the government also had to protect the weak, vulnerable members of society, like children, and look after the poor. But Bentham recognised that government action had to be justified and kept to the minimum necessary. In order to do this and prevent government encroaching on the freedom of the majority, every law and government organisation should be subject to a test of 'utility', i.e. What is it for? What use is it? Is it effective? Does it work? If institutions weren't working, they should be reformed.

It followed that Utilitarians stressed the need for thorough investigation, precise laws and effective enforcement. One of the problems to which Bentham and his followers applied their theory of **Utilitarianism** was that of poverty. This is the subject of the next section. But, first we need to examine pressure for reform from another quarter; the humanitarians.

Humanitarianism

Humanitarians included Whig, Tory and Radical MPs as well as many people outside Parliament. They campaigned to alleviate the harsh working conditions in the mines and factories, especially for women and children. Humanitarianism was inspired by Christian beliefs and many saw it as their Christian duty to relieve the suffering of the downtrodden, weaker members of society. They were known as **evangelical Christians**. One of the most prominent evangelical Christians was William Wilberforce, who led the campaign against slavery. In 1833, Parliament abolished slavery in the British Empire (which mainly meant the West Indies). The government paid out £20 million in compensation to the slave-owners for their loss of 'property'. This amount was about half what was spent on running the country each year.

Key question
What were the key ideas of Utilitarianism?

Key term

Utilitarianism
A set of ideas developed by Jeremy Bentham who argued that government should be judged on its ability to promote 'the greatest happiness of the greatest number'.

Key question
What were the key ideas of Humanitarianism?

Key terms

Humanitarianism
Working for the welfare of human beings, e.g. to reduce suffering.

Evangelical Christians
Christians who believed that God called them to devote their time to good causes. They believed that better social conditions would give dignity to the poor and make them more responsive to religion.

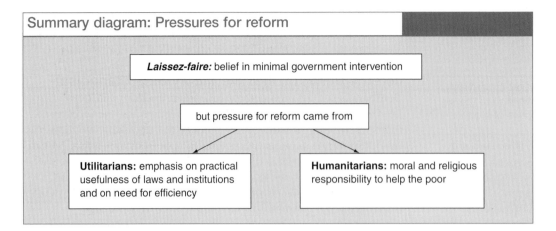

Summary diagram: Pressures for reform

Laissez-faire: belief in minimal government intervention

but pressure for reform came from

Utilitarians: emphasis on practical usefulness of laws and institutions and on need for efficiency

Humanitarians: moral and religious responsibility to help the poor

2 | The Old Poor Law

In the nineteenth century, people often referred to the '**labouring poor**', meaning all those who earned a living by manual labour (as opposed to shopkeepers, clerks, merchants, doctors, lawyers, landowners, etc.). They made up the majority of the population and all of them lived in poverty or fear of poverty. In the countryside, the workers depended on the climate (as well as their landlord) and a poor harvest carried the threat of starvation. In the cities, they were dependent on market forces; the loss of foreign markets and a depression in trade could mean a prolonged period of unemployment. While the skilled and better-off workers could manage to save *some* money while they were working, most of the poor earned only just enough to survive. As a result, being without a job meant hunger. There were no unemployment benefits, old-age pensions or National Health Service so most working families expected to face hardship at some time in their lives.

Those who could not afford to look after themselves – which included many of the old, sick, disabled and orphans, as well as the unemployed – often had to fall back on the '**poor relief**' provided by the parish. The parish was the main unit of local government and there were over 15,000 of them. Since Elizabethan times, the Poor Law had made the parish responsible for care of the poor.

Poor relief was paid for by the propertied classes through local taxes, called the poor rates, and was administered by parish **overseers**. For those who could not look after themselves in their own homes, such as some of the elderly and the disabled, relief was provided in a local poorhouse, or workhouse. This was known as 'indoor relief'. But most were given 'outdoor relief' and did not have to enter the workhouse. This could be in the form of food, clothing or money. Those who depended on poor relief were known as '**paupers**'. Most of the labouring poor faced the prospect of becoming paupers at some time in their lives.

In the early nineteenth century, more and more people were seeking poor relief and the costs were rising (as you can see in

Key question
Who were the poor and how were they cared for?

Key terms

Labouring poor
All those who earned their living by manual labour.

Poor relief
Support provided for the poor whether inside a workhouse ('indoor relief') or outside, in the form of money, food or clothing ('outdoor relief').

Overseers
The people appointed in the parish to collect the poor rate and decide how it was spent.

Paupers
Those who received benefits through the Poor Law system.

Figure 6.1). The main reason was rapid population growth. A series of poor harvests or a trade depression could also increase the pressure on the Poor Law authorities. There was much variation in how poor relief was provided and the system could be adapted to suit local circumstances. In some parishes, those claiming poor relief were obliged to enter the workhouse. However, in most, outdoor relief was more common.

One particular parish, Speenhamland in Berkshire, was faced with the challenge of providing for people who were employed (as farm labourers), but whose wages were so low that they could not support their families. In 1795 the Speenhamland authorities decided to top up these people's wages with allowances. The size of the allowance was based on the price of bread, which was the main foodstuff, and on the size of the family. The bigger the family, the bigger the allowance paid by the parish overseers. This seemed just and fair; it was geared to the needs of the poor and it suited local circumstances.

Opposition to the Poor Law

The practice of topping up wages was followed by a number of other parishes in the south of England and it became known as the **Speenhamland system**. It did, however, come in for mounting criticism. It was criticised for allowing farmers to pay their workers low wages in the knowledge that their pay would be supplemented by the Poor Law authorities. This, in turn, meant that other farmers and ratepayers had to pay higher rates. But, above all, it was criticised for encouraging laziness and large families among the labouring poor. Critics claimed that men did not have to work particularly hard if they knew that their wages would be topped up. They said that this encouraged people to have large families at a time when it was feared that population was rising faster than food production. The system was encouraging the labouring poor to depend on parish relief rather than on their own efforts. For that reason it was immoral as well as costly.

Figure 6.1: Cost of the Poor Rate in England.

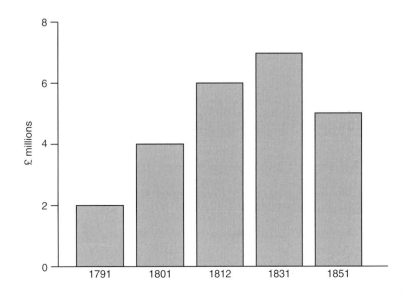

It was the rising cost of poor relief (see Figure 6.1) that did most to increase opposition and calls for reform. Some of the highest increases in the cost of providing poor relief were in the agricultural, southern counties of England, yet it was here that most of the outbreaks of violence, known as the Swing riots, occurred in 1830–1 (see pages 46–7). The governing classes were prepared to pay a certain price, in the form of the poor rates, for social stability and the prevention of disorder. However, if a higher bill for poor relief led to riots then, they argued, the whole system was not working and should be reformed.

When the Whigs came to power in 1830, they were swift to punish the Swing rioters. They also responded to the calls for reform of the Poor Law that were coming from ratepayers and, in particular, from the Benthamites. In 1832, they established a Commission (or committee) to investigate and make recommendations for reform of the system.

Key date

Poor Law Commission set up: 1832

The leading Commissioners were Edwin Chadwick, a Utilitarian and friend of Jeremy Bentham, and Nassau Senior, an Oxford professor who was a keen supporter of *laissez-faire* economics. These men and their fellow Commissioners sent out questionnaires and visited over 3000 parishes to collect first-hand reports. The evidence collected filled several volumes. This was by far the fullest survey that had ever been carried out by government. It provided Chadwick and Senior with all the evidence they needed. They had known what they wanted all along. Now they had the evidence to support the recommendations they had already decided on.

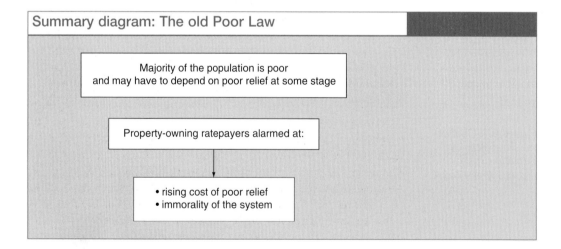

Summary diagram: The old Poor Law

Majority of the population is poor and may have to depend on poor relief at some stage

Property-owning ratepayers alarmed at:

• rising cost of poor relief
• immorality of the system

3 | The Poor Law Amendment Act 1834

The recommendations made in the report were based on the following principles:

Key question
What were the recommendations of the Poor Law Commission?

• *the 'workhouse test'*: all 'outdoor relief' to be abolished and poor relief to be available only in workhouses

- *'less eligibility'*: conditions in the workhouse to be 'less eligible' (less pleasant) than those of the poorest paid worker outside; this would deter all but the most needy
- *centralisation*: the administration of poor relief to be the same everywhere or else paupers would simply go where conditions were more lenient; this could be achieved only through a centralised system.

These principles would satisfy the Utilitarian demand for efficiency and the *laissez-faire* demand for minimum government interference in the economy. If the recommendations were translated into law, employers would no longer be able to keep wages low in the belief that the Poor Law authorities would top them up. Furthermore, the poor would be encouraged to work harder, to do all they could to earn a wage and remain independent. They would become more self-reliant and less likely to live off the parish. The whole British economy would benefit. In short, these recommendations would satisfy both the economic and the moral arguments for reform.

The outcome of the Commission's recommendations

The Poor Law Amendment Act carried out the recommendations of the Commission report. It also stated that:

- a Poor Law Commission, based in London, would be established with Chadwick as its secretary
- parishes would be grouped together, in Poor Law Unions, each with its own workhouse, and locally elected **Guardians** would replace the unelected overseers
- Assistant Commissioners would be appointed to oversee the enforcement of the law in the regions.

The Act received wide support in Parliament. The middle classes, who were now more represented in the Reformed Parliament, were just as supportive of this measure as the landed classes. But there was one aspect that was not so popular among the latter: the centralised nature of the system. Most government was local government at this time and local independence was jealously guarded. Local landowners, in the countryside, and local businessmen, in the urban areas, continued to control the administration of poor relief. They resented the directives and instructions that poured out of London, mainly from Chadwick.

As the leading Utilitarian (Bentham died in 1832), Chadwick wanted to use the Commission to set and maintain uniform standards throughout the country. He wanted to cut out the inefficiency that resulted from local variations, but the Poor Law Guardians generally believed that they were in a better position to decide how the Poor Law should be administered in their areas and they hated what they saw as unnecessary interference from London.

Key term

Guardians
Officials to be responsible for the administration of poor relief locally. In practice, many of the old overseers were elected as Guardians.

The impact of the new Poor Law

Over the years the cost of poor relief decreased, as shown in Figure 6.1 (see page 91). In this way, the new law achieved one of its main objectives and pleased most the propertied classes who paid the poor rates. By the end of 1839, the majority of the country's 15,000 parishes had been grouped into nearly 600 Poor Law Unions.

However, the new system was hated by many of the 'labouring poor' and their humanitarian supporters, both inside and outside Parliament. The main criticisms were:

Key question
How successful was the new Poor Law?

- the Poor Law report and the Act focused too heavily on the able-bodied poor, who the law makers felt to be 'undeserving', at the expense of the 'deserving poor' – the old, the sick, the disabled, etc.
- the report had exaggerated the extent to which the Speenhamland system was practised
- the report and the Act overlooked the problems of those of the unemployed who genuinely sought work to support themselves and their families; the central concept, that poverty was the fault of the poor, was seen as degrading
- the enforcement of the principle of 'less eligibility' meant that life in the workhouse was to be extremely harsh.

Conditions in the workhouse

Many of the most vulnerable members of society, those who could not help themselves, were probably better housed and better fed than those who were 'merely poor' outside the workhouse. But workhouse regulations were seen by the poor as unjust and punitive because:

Key question
What was life like for those in the workhouse?

- the sexes were separated
- families were split up
- inmates wore uniforms, like prisoners
- labour, for the able-bodied, was hard and repetitive
- food was monotonous and had to be eaten in silence.

The harshest aspects of the workhouse regime were not always enforced. The old and orphaned were often treated more kindly. In practice, much depended on the particular workhouse masters. Some of them were far more harsh than the Commissioners intended. Some, for instance, singled out unmarried mothers for special treatment (such as being separated at meal times or having to wear a special uniform) and, where there were scandals, as in the **Andover workhouse**, it was more a case of local abuse by the workhouse master than the fault of the Poor Law Commission. After all, there were only a small number of Assistant Commissioners to see that the standards set in London were enforced all over the country.

Nevertheless, it was the psychological hardships – the boredom, the monotony and the petty rules – which were most hated. The workhouse was a dreaded and humiliating experience for many. It

Key term

Andover workhouse
In 1846, paupers in the Andover workhouse, who had been set the task of crushing animal bones for fertiliser, were so hungry that they had been found gnawing the bones in order to eat the marrow.

> **Regulations governing life in the Southampton Workhouse 1841**
>
> II That the Master read or cause to be read prayers every morning before breakfast, and every evening after Supper
>
> VI That the Master and Mistress rise themselves and cause all under their care, who are well, to rise at seven o'clock in the winter and at six in the summer
>
> VIII That all go to bed and all candles be carefully extinguished by eight o'clock in the winter and in the summer all shall be in bed before nine
>
> IX That they have their breakfast in the winter at eight and in the summer at seven in the morning, their dinner always at twelve and their supper at six in the winter and at seven in the summer
>
> X That no waste be made of bread, beer or meat, but what is left be referred for another meal
>
> XIV That if any swear, lie or be guilty of any scandalous practice, they be punished accordingly

certainly acted as a deterrent to all but the most desperate. This was, after all, the intention of the government.

Opposition to the new Poor Law

Key question
How effective was the Anti-Poor Law movement?

It is not surprising, then, that the new workhouses earned the nickname of '**Bastilles**'. Nor is it surprising that great shame was attached to being on poor relief, especially if it meant having to go into the workhouse.

At first, the Poor Law Commission concentrated on putting the new system into practice in the largely rural, southern counties. There was considerable opposition and some outbreaks of violence but, by mid-1836, the new system was operating across the agricultural southern counties. However, when the new Poor Law was implemented in the industrial north, from 1837 onwards, there was widespread and organised opposition.

The new Poor Law had been largely based on the experience and evidence collected from rural areas, where the majority of the population still lived. The experience of industrial areas was very different and ill-understood by those who had framed the Act. These areas, especially the textile towns of Lancashire and Yorkshire, were highly dependent on exports so that, if there was a slump in trade, thousands could be thrown out of work. Sometimes, the period of unemployment might only be for a short time but, at other times, as in 1837–8, it could last for several months. In these circumstances, unemployment was certainly not the fault of the workers. Nor could they all be accommodated in workhouses. It was both fairer and cheaper to provide outdoor relief.

Key term

'Bastilles'
Named after the Parisian prison, liberated in the French Revolution, which was seen as a symbol of oppression. Workhouses were often surrounded by high walls and were compared to prisons by their opponents.

Key date

Introduction of the new Poor Law in the North: 1837

Anti-Poor Law poster, drawn in 1837 when the new Poor Law was first introduced in the north of England. The handwritten heading is: 'The New Poor Law, with a description of the new workhouses. Look at the picture. See.'

The Poor Law authorities in the industrial towns resented and ignored the new Poor Law regulations. They were also often sympathetic to the workers. In some cases, they supported the resistance of the Anti-Poor Law movement that spread across the industrial north of England. Attempts to put the new Poor Law into practice in the north were obstructed, often by organised violence. Sometimes troops were brought in to restore order. By 1839 the agitation had died down and much of the momentum of the resistance was being channelled into the Chartist movement (which is examined in the next chapter).

The outdoor labour test

Nevertheless, the opposition did achieve some success. The Poor Law Commissioners eventually backed down and agreed to allow outdoor relief. Instead of insisting on the workhouse test for all paupers (i.e. they could only receive poor relief if they were willing to enter the workhouse), they accepted the Outdoor Labour Test whereby paupers could receive outdoor relief in return for doing work provided by the Poor Law union.

In fact, outdoor relief continued to be the main form of poor relief in the country as a whole. Certainly, for many of the old and sick, help was provided in the home as it was seen to be more humane. Furthermore, outdoor relief was cheaper.

The lasting influence of the new Poor Law

The Poor Law Amendment Act of 1834 was to be the most important piece of social legislation enacted in the whole of the nineteenth century. It established the policy that was to shape the practice of the Poor Law for the rest of the century. Furthermore, it reinforced what was to remain the prevailing view of poverty among the governing classes in Victorian Britain: that poverty was largely an individual's personal failing and that 'self-help' was the way out.

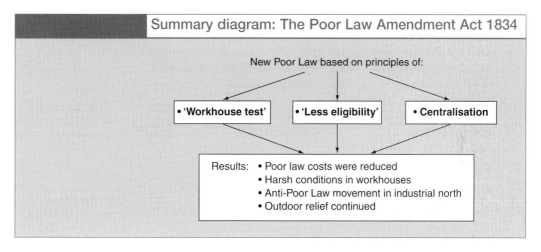

Summary diagram: The Poor Law Amendment Act 1834

New Poor Law based on principles of:

- 'Workhouse test'
- 'Less eligibility'
- Centralisation

Results:
- Poor law costs were reduced
- Harsh conditions in workhouses
- Anti-Poor Law movement in industrial north
- Outdoor relief continued

4 | Factory Reform

Key question
Who supported factory reform and why?

Most of the labouring poor, men, women and children, were used to working long hours. They had traditionally done so in the countryside and at home. But, working at home, under the domestic system (see page 5), they had been able to work at their own pace. In contrast, in the factories, the hours were long, monotonous and imposed by the employer, and reinforced by factory bells and regulations. Furthermore, much of the labour was provided by women and children so that their menfolk could no longer control and protect them as they had done under the domestic system.

Key term

Ten Hours Movement
A campaign started in 1830 for a 10-hour day for all workers. Support for the movement was organised through Short Time Committees, mostly made up of factory workers.

Key date
Start of the Ten Hours Movement: 1830

The Ten Hours Movement

Campaigns for factory reform developed in the early nineteenth century. There had been attempts, before 1830, to restrict the working hours of children but they had not been very effective. In 1830, the **Ten Hours Movement** was established. Its aim was to campaign for a 10-hour day for all workers, both children and adults. The movement was centred in the predominantly textile-producing areas of Lancashire and Yorkshire. Pamphlets and petitions were produced and 'missionaries' [enthusiasts] travelled round the industrial areas to publicise evidence of the brutal exploitation of children.

Factory reform attracted a wide range of support, not only from the working classes but also from humanitarians among the landed and industrial middle classes. Supporters included a number of so-called Tory radicals, the best known of whom was **Richard Oastler**, the manager of a large landed estate in Yorkshire. He believed that the ruling classes had a moral responsibility to protect the weak and vulnerable. In 1830, he sent a letter to the *Leeds Mercury* entitled 'Yorkshire slavery'. In this letter he reminded several local factory owners, who were enthusiastic supporters of the anti-slavery movement, that they did not need to go to the West Indies to discover slavery, but could find it in their own factories.

Other prominent reformers were John Fielden and Michael Sadler. Fielden was a factory owner who believed that decent wages and reasonable hours would make factory workers healthier and more productive. Sadler was a Tory MP. In 1832 he chaired a House of Commons committee that collected evidence from factory districts and recommended a bill to introduce a 10-hour day for all textile factories. Parliament was not convinced. Sadler was known to be a keen reformer and his evidence was felt to be one-sided, too dependent on support from the Ten Hours Movement.

Richard Oastler — Key term
One of the leaders of the Ten Hours Movement. He opposed universal suffrage and trade unions, but believed that the rich and powerful had a duty to look after the poor and the weak. He opposed the new Poor Law and saw the workhouses as inhumane.

Royal Commission into Employment of Children in Factories: 1833 — Key date

Key question
What were the main terms of the 1833 Factory Act?

The Factory Act 1833

Parliament believed that more employers should be consulted and, in 1833, appointed a Royal Commission with Edwin Chadwick as chairman. This Commission based its conclusions on grounds of efficiency rather than humanitarianism. The report argued that tired, unhealthy workers were not productive. It accepted the employers' opposition to State intervention and upheld *laissez-faire* principles. However, it argued that children were not free to decide what was in their own best interests and therefore needed protection. The result was the Factory Act of 1833.

The Act applied only to textile factories, or mills, and stated:

- no children under nine years of age to be employed
- children aged 9–12 years to work a maximum of 9 hours a day (and no more than 48 hours a week)
- young people 13–18 years to work a maximum of 12 hours a day (and no more than 68 hours a week)
- children aged 9–11 years to receive two hours' schooling a day.

As with the new Poor Law, the influence of the Utilitarians was clear in the way the investigation was conducted and inspectors were appointed to ensure that the Act was carried out. The principle of *laissez-faire* was upheld in restricting government intervention in the employer–employee relationship, but both Utilitarian and humanitarian principles were followed in protecting those who were seen as not being 'free agents': children needed to be protected.

Oastler and supporters of the Ten Hours Movement hoped that the restriction on children's hours would lead to a limit on the hours of the adults they worked alongside. This was because work done by adults often depended on different types of work done by children. But the employers got round this by employing the children in shifts. There was to be no legal restriction on the hours that men worked until the end of the century: they were 'free agents' and an economy run largely along *laissez-faire* lines would enable Britain to remain competitive. If men's working hours were restricted, employers' profits would fall and workers would be laid off. This was the view of most of the employing classes who dominated Parliament.

The impact of the Act

Key question
How effective was the 1833 Factory Act?

The terms of the Act were widely ignored. There were only four inspectors for the whole country, even though they were able to appoint assistants. Many employers continued to make use of cheap child labour and many parents wanted their children to bring in much-needed income. It was not only the bosses who resented government interference. Also, it was difficult for the inspectors to decide on children's ages; it was only from 1836 onwards that official records of births (and marriages and deaths) were kept.

Nevertheless, as the inspectors became more familiar with factory conditions, they were able to take more employers to court for breaking the law. From 1833 to 1855 most of the prosecutions in Lancashire and West Yorkshire were successful. A start had been made and the foundations laid for further legislation in the 1840s.

Factory reform in the 1840s

Key question
What further legislation was passed in the 1840s?

Further legislation was passed in the 1840s:

- *1842 Mines Act*: women, girls and boys under 10 years of age not to work below ground in coal mines.
- *1844 Factory Act*: women restricted to 12 hours work a day, children under 13 years of age limited to six and a half hours work a day, and schooling increased to 3 hours a day; dangerous machinery to be fenced in.
- *1847 Ten Hours Act*: women and young people limited to 10 hours a day.

A girl dragging coal underground. Drawings like this were reproduced in the 1842 report on the employment of children in mines. In the days before photography, such drawings were used as visual evidence of conditions in the mines. They had great propaganda value as they shocked the MPs.

We have already noted the influence of the Utilitarians in passing factory reform. The impact of evangelical Christians was also evident: for them, factory reform was moral reform. Factories and mines were seen as breeding grounds of immorality, hence the linking of reform with education. In 1842, those serving on the Commission investigating the coal mines were shocked to find that women worked underground, stripped to the waist, cutting coal alongside the men. They considered this to be a dangerous sexual temptation. The laws of 1842 and 1844, which protected women at work, were as much about defining 'acceptable' moral standards as they were about improving working conditions.

Despite the difficulties of enforcing factory reform, much progress had been made, largely as a result of the dedication of several key reformers. But it is worth remembering that these reforms applied only to textile factories and coal mines. They did not extend to other factories until much later in the nineteenth century.

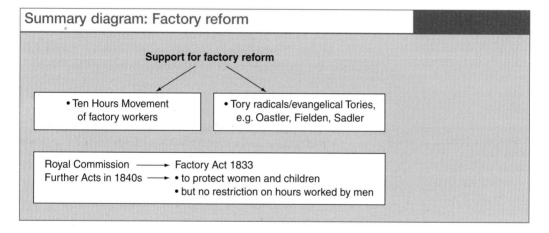

Summary diagram: Factory reform

5 | Reform of Local Government and the Church

Key question
Why was local government reformed?

Reform of local government was very much a follow-up to the reform of Parliament, although it was not completed until 1835. It was based on the report of another Royal Commission, which the Whigs set up in 1833. One of the Commission's main figures was the Whig MP and Utilitarian, Joseph Parkes.

Over previous centuries many towns had been granted charters, which gave them the right to set up town corporations (or town councils). As with parliamentary boroughs, some were very small whereas large, new towns like Manchester, Birmingham and Leeds had no charters and thus no corporation, or town council. The right to vote for corporations was very limited and local government was often in the hands of a small, self-electing group, more often Tory than Whig.

The Whigs wanted to enfranchise the new middle classes, so that they could all vote for the election of town councils, and thus make those councils more efficient. They also wanted to improve law and order in the increasingly undisciplined large towns.

The Municipal Corporations Act 1835

The main terms of the **Municipal Corporations** Act 1835 were:

- 178 corporations were abolished and replaced by elected town councils
- all those who paid local rates (taxes) were to have the vote
- each council would elect its own mayor and aldermen (officials)
- the councils were to organise local police forces
- large towns without corporations could apply for the right to elect their own councils. Manchester and Birmingham were the first new town councils to be established.

There was now a uniform system of elected town councils throughout the country. The franchise was limited to the ratepayers, which effectively meant property owners, since rates were based on property. In other words, it was largely the middle classes who benefited – as in the 1832 reform of Parliament. Most of the working classes were excluded. The first town council elected under the new Act was in Leicester and was made up almost entirely of local traders, shopkeepers and bankers with a few 'professionals' such as doctors.

The new town councils generally were keen to improve law and order and to combat crime. Not surprisingly, however, they were dominated by people who believed in *laissez-faire* ideas and were reluctant to spend their own and other ratepayers' money dealing with disease and providing clean water and sewerage.

Reform of the Church of England

In the 1832 Reform Act the Whig government removed the worst of the abuses in the parliamentary system. They also set out to do the same for the Church of England. As you know from Chapter 3 (page 42), this was the official, State Church that had been established in the sixteenth century.

The Church was politically powerful. The king was Head of the Church of England and all the bishops were members of the House of Lords (as they are today). The Church was also rich. It owned much land and had the right to raise a tax, called the church rate, from all who owned land in its parishes and to demand a **tithe**.

During the Reform crisis of 1831–2 the Church came in for a lot of criticism, especially when the bishops in the House of Lords voted against the Reform Bill. During the election held after Reform, there was much demand for reform of the Church. The main criticisms were:

- the Church was out of touch with society, especially with the needs of the urban working class
- there was a big gap between the rich lifestyle that bishops were said to enjoy and that of the poorest parish clergy
- some clergy were in charge of, and received income for, several parishes

Key question
What were the main terms of the Act?

Key terms

Municipal corporation
'Municipal' refers to local government. 'Corporation' means a town council.

Tithe
A one-tenth tax of a person's income, payable to the Church.

Key question
Why did the Church need to be reformed?

- people who were not members of the Church of England – such as Catholics and Protestant Nonconformists (see page 11) – had to pay church rates for the upkeep of a Church to which they did not belong.

Before the Whigs had time to carry out any reform of the Church, they were replaced by a Tory government, led by Robert Peel, in 1834. Peel's government lasted only a few months, but it set up an **Ecclesiastical** Commission to recommend reforms. This body was made up of churchmen and of government officials and it was to remain permanent, with the job of supervising changes and recommending further reforms.

Most of the recommendations of the Ecclesiastical Commission became law when the Whigs returned to power in 1835. The main reforms were:

- the creation of two new **dioceses**, in Manchester and in Yorkshire, largely to serve the needs of new, industrial areas
- some redistribution of Church money to poorer clergy and to build new churches in the cities
- payment of tithes became a money payment, which was seen as less burdensome
- clergy could hold no more than two parishes.

These reforms were seen as practical improvements and were widely supported.

Support for Nonconformists and Catholics

There were also changes that affected Nonconformists and Catholics:

- The Marriage Act 1836 allowed Nonconformists and Catholics to marry in their own churches as long as they had a licence.
- London University, which admitted non-**Anglicans** (unlike Oxford and Cambridge), was granted the right to award degrees to its students.
- The government took over responsibility for keeping a register of all births, marriages and deaths. Previously this had been done in the parishes of the Church of England. Now it would be done for everyone, not just members of the Church of England.

In Ireland, Catholics continued to resent and oppose the domination of the Anglican **Church of Ireland**. Over 90 per cent of the population of Ireland was Catholic yet they still had to pay tithes and church rates to support 22 bishops and 2500 parishes of the Church of Ireland. A 'tithe war' had started in 1831 in which Catholics refused to pay tithes for the upkeep of the Church of Ireland. Although the Whigs refused to abolish tithes, they did, in 1833, pass an Act which:

- reduced the number of bishops to 12
- abolished the church rates
- abolished parishes where there were no Anglican churchgoers.

Key terms

Ecclesiastical
Concerning the Church.

Dioceses
Areas into which the country was divided for church purposes. Each diocese had a bishop at its head.

Anglicans
Members of the Church of England.

Church of Ireland
Effectively the Irish branch of the Church of England.

Key dates

Marriage Act allowed Nonconformists and Catholics to marry in their own churches: 1836

Reform of the Church of Ireland: 1833

The whole issue of the Church of Ireland and Irish affairs caused great problems for the Whigs in the 1830s and was a major cause of their decline and eventual defeat in 1841.

Summary diagram: Reform of local government and the Church

Municipal Corporation Act was passed to:

- abolish old, corrupt corporations
- have town councils elected by all the ratepayers
- incorporate new towns

Church reform was passed to:

- set up the Ecclesiastical Commission
- redistribute money to poorer clergy and the new cities
- allow Catholics and Nonconformists to get married in their own churches
- reduce the financial burden of the Church of Ireland on the Irish people

---

6 | The Decline of the Whigs and the 1841 Election

Key question
What led to the resignation of the Whigs in 1834?

When the Whigs reformed the Church of Ireland in 1833 they saved money. That left the question of what to do with this money. The Whig minister, Lord John Russell, suggested that some of the savings be used for non-Church purposes such as setting up more schools in Ireland. He hoped this might reduce anti-English feeling. However, his proposal caused uproar – in the Church, among the Tories and even among some of Russell's fellow Whigs. The proposal was portrayed as an attack on the property of the Anglican Church, even as 'burglary'. Some even said that it threatened the Union of Great Britain and Ireland.

Key date
Whigs forced to resign: November 1834

Four members of the Whig cabinet resigned (two of them later joined the Tories) and, a few months later, so too did Earl Grey. Already exhausted by the struggle for reform in 1832, he was tired of the splits within his government. Lord Melbourne became Prime Minister. But the political turmoil did not die down. The king did not like Melbourne and he detested Russell and his proposal. In November 1834 he secured the resignation of the Whig government and asked Wellington to form a Tory government.

Peel becomes Prime Minister 1834

Key question
What was the significance of the Tamworth Manifesto?

Wellington said that only Peel could lead a Tory government. Peel, however, was on holiday in Italy. Messages were sent by horse to Peel and three weeks later he returned to become Prime Minister. As the Tories were in a minority in the House of

Commons, Peel asked the king to dissolve Parliament so that an election could be held. It was at this time that Peel issued what has become known as the Tamworth Manifesto. It was an open letter to the electors in his constituency of Tamworth but it was written with a wider audience in mind and was released to the press.

The Tamworth Manifesto 1834

The manifesto was Peel's attempt to show the new electorate that the Tories had moved on and were no longer the weak and backward-looking party they seemed to be in 1832. In it he said: 'I consider the Reform Bill a final settlement', i.e. he accepted it. Then he went on to promise:

- 'the correction of proved abuses and the redress of real grievances'
- 'the support of public credit – the enforcement of strict economy', i.e. good financial management
- 'the just and impartial consideration of what is due to all interests – agricultural, manufacturing and commercial' – i.e. that his government would rule on behalf of all classes, not just the landed.

It was also at this time that the term '**Conservative**' came to be used to refer to Peel's party. In effect, the Tory party was being given a new image. In the manifesto Peel promised to reform abuses, but he was also keen to show that he would *conserve* 'established institutions' such as the Church at a time when the Whigs appeared to be less reliable. This was skilful use of propaganda on Peel's part.

In the election of January 1835 the Conservatives regained nearly 100 of the seats they had lost in 1832, but they still had 100 fewer than the Whigs. However, they stayed in power for a few months. They set up the Ecclesiastical Commission and, above all, showed that they were a realistic alternative to the Whigs. They proved that they were not the broken party that some Whigs had assumed they were after 1832.

However, in February 1835, the Whigs held a meeting with Radical and Irish MPs in which they agreed to unite and defeat the Conservatives in Parliament. This was the so-called **Lichfield House Compact**. The Whigs now had a large majority and Peel was forced to resign in April 1835.

The decline of the Whigs 1835–41

The Whigs had passed several major reforms between 1832 and 1835. These included factory reform, the new Poor Law and reform of local government. Peel, although in opposition, had supported much Whig reform. However, in the second half of the 1830s, the Whigs passed much less reform. They seemed to run out of steam and Lord Melbourne was one of the least dynamic Prime Ministers there has ever been. However, it was not lack of reform so much as fear of more reform that led to a decline in support for the Whigs in Parliament. The reason for this was that

Conservative
Came into use at the time of the Tamworth Manifesto when Peel promised that he would *conserve* the nation's institutions. Nevertheless, the term 'Tory' continued to be used as well.

Lichfield House Compact
Meeting of Whigs, Radicals and Irish MPs held at the house of Lord Lichfield in February 1835. They agreed to form an alliance to defeat Peel's Conservative government.

Peel was Prime Minister of a Tory/Conservative government: December 1834 to April 1835

Key question
What weakened the Whig government in the later 1830s?

the Whigs appeared to be dependent on the support of Radicals and the Irish in Parliament. At least, that is how the Conservatives portrayed the situation.

In Parliament there was a small number of Radical MPs who wanted the secret ballot for elections and an extension of the franchise. However, they were never a strong or united group. More problematical for the Whigs were the 30 or 40 Irish MPs led by Daniel O'Connell. After the passing of Catholic Emancipation in 1829 (see pages 42–4), Catholics could become MPs and they now formed a group in Parliament that was committed to repeal of the Act of Union between Britain and Ireland. The Irish MPs were not campaigning for complete independence, but for the restoration of the Irish Parliament in Dublin that had been ended by the Union in 1800.

The Whigs were not prepared to go that far but they attempted to pacify the Irish by carrying out mild reforms such as reducing the cost of maintaining the Anglican Church of Ireland. They had done this in 1833. But, as we know, when Lord Russell suggested that some of the wealth of the Anglican Church of Ireland be used for schools (i.e. non-Church purposes), their opponents were horrified and the Cabinet was split.

Then, after the Lichfield House Compact in 1835 (see page 104), the Conservatives regularly accused the Whigs of being swayed by their Irish and Radical allies. In fact, the Whigs did not carry out the radical reforms that these two groups wanted, but Peel and his party played on the electorate's fears that they *would* do so. The Conservatives said that the Whigs could not be trusted to defend the Church of England. *The Times* joined in the attack: in 1836, it accused Melbourne of undermining 'the Protestant monarchy of Great Britain'.

King William died and was succeeded by Queen Victoria: 1837

Key date

In 1837 King William IV died and was succeeded by the young Queen Victoria. At that time a general election had to be held when a new monarch ascended the throne. In the election the Whigs secured more seats than the Conservatives, but their majority was now very small and they became more dependent on the support of the Irish and Radical MPs in Parliament. This played into the hands of Peel and the Conservatives. They said that the Irish and Radical tail was wagging the Whig dog.

The 1841 election

Key question
Why did the Conservatives win the 1841 election?

Problems piled up for the Whigs in the late 1830s. In 1837 and 1838 there were bad harvests, hunger and hardship. Foreign trade was hit by economic depression in Europe and unemployment increased. There was already widespread opposition to the new Poor Law in the industrial north of England. This now merged into the working-class movement known as Chartism (see Chapter 7) and it spread to many parts of Britain. Despite the use of troops and the new police forces, there were disturbances in many areas. The Conservatives accused the Whigs of being unable to maintain law and order.

With trade hit by depression, the government gained less money from tariffs and other taxes on goods. The government went into debt and the Conservatives blamed the Whigs for failing to balance the national budget.

In 1841 the Conservatives defeated the Whigs in a vote in Parliament and an election was called. During the election campaign Lord Russell proposed a change to the Corn Laws (see page 17). This may have pleased the urban voters in the industrial areas, but it horrified the landed classes. The Conservatives pounced, claiming that the Whigs were planning complete repeal of the Corn Laws. Not only was the Church in danger from the Whigs, claimed the Conservatives, but now British agriculture and the landed classes were under threat. If the Whigs won the election, Britain would be flooded with cheap foreign grain and the farmers would go out of business.

As it was, the Whigs won most of the parliamentary seats in the large towns and cities but, overall, it was a Conservative victory in 1841. Peel's party convinced the voters that they would form a stronger, more competent government. Above all, the Conservatives won back nearly all the rural, county seats that they had lost when they opposed parliamentary reform in 1831–2. In other words, their victory was largely based in old Tory England, in the landed, Anglican shires.

> **Key date**
>
> Conservatives won the general election: 1841

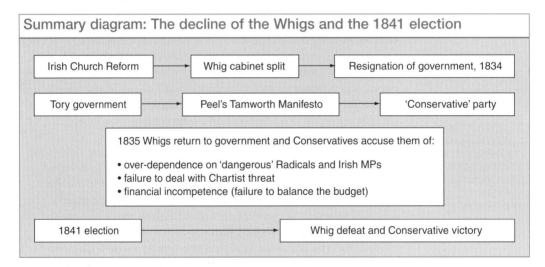

Summary diagram: The decline of the Whigs and the 1841 election

Irish Church Reform → Whig cabinet split → Resignation of government, 1834

Tory government → Peel's Tamworth Manifesto → 'Conservative' party

1835 Whigs return to government and Conservatives accuse them of:
- over-dependence on 'dangerous' Radicals and Irish MPs
- failure to deal with Chartist threat
- financial incompetence (failure to balance the budget)

1841 election → Whig defeat and Conservative victory

Study Guide: AS Questions

In the style of AQA

Study the following source material and then answer the questions that follow.

From: Collier and Pedley, Britain 1815–51: Protest and Reform, 2001.

The Swing riots of 1830–1 provided the turning point in attitudes towards the poor. The level of unrest was interpreted by the new Whig government led by Earl Grey as evidence of the failure of the old Poor Law.

(a) Comment on the 'Swing riots' in the context of the years before 1834. (3 marks)

(b) Explain why there was so much pressure to reform the Poor Law in 1834. (7 marks)

(c) How successful were the Whig domestic reforms of the period 1833 to 1841? (15 marks)

Exam tips

The cross-references are intended to take you straight to the material that will help you to answer the questions.

(a) Question **(a)** should only need three or four sentences to answer this short question. You should:

- describe key features of these rural riots, using your own knowledge (pages 46–7)
- refer to the source and give a brief explanation of how and why the riots were seen 'as evidence of the failure of the old Poor Law'.

(b) In question **(b)** you should explain very briefly how the old Poor Law worked (pages 90–2):

- indoor relief (workhouse) and outdoor relief
- how it was financed, i.e. local rates paid by property-owning classes.

    This should lead on to pressures for reform which will include the issue of cost; explain:

- how poor rates had risen in the years leading up to 1834
- the part of the Speenhamland system in this
- why Swing riots were 'the turning point', to use the phrase from the source, e.g. riots were concentrated in rural south yet that was where costs had risen most.

    Then you should explore the *moral* issue:

- how outdoor relief was seen to encourage laziness and large families among the poor, especially where Speenhamland system was practised
- how a system that acted as more of a deterrent was sought to make the poor more independent and self-reliant.

    This should lead on to some explanation of the influence of Utilitarians like Chadwick, who wanted to produce a system that deterred the poor from seeking poor relief, thus dealing with both moral and cost issues. Try to link the factors and avoid a 'shopping list' of points in your answer. To achieve 6–7 marks, you need to prioritise, interlink or draw conclusions from the factors you present.

(c) For question **(c)** the main reforms are likely to be:

- 1833 Factory Act
- 1834 Poor Law Amendment Act
- 1835 Municipal Corporations Act

with the Poor Law receiving most attention because of its importance. Others might include: Church reform and abolition of slavery. However, you will need to prioritise and the omission of some lesser reforms will not be penalised. Success will need to be measured in different ways, e.g. for the new *Poor Law*:

- it had wide support in Parliament and among most of the property-owning classes who financed poor relief
- new Poor Law reduced costs and deterred many of the poor from claiming relief because of the threat of the workhouse, therefore a success
- on the other hand, it aroused anger, organised opposition and contributed to Chartism, all of which can be interpreted as evidence of failure
- outdoor relief continued to be main form of relief, so a prime objective of the reformers was not achieved.

You could argue that it was largely a success from a Utilitarian perspective but not from a humanitarian one. *Factory reform* has elements of both success and failure, depending again on criteria used to judge it. Humanitarians might see it as only a minor success, as not covering adults and very few inspectors were appointed to see that it was enforced. Believers in *laissez-faire* might see it as necessary protection for the young and an undoubted success in that it did not affect terms of employment for adults. Your conclusion will need to make an overall judgement, perhaps explaining the comparative lack of reform and ineffectiveness of Whig government in the years of economic depression at the end of the decade.

In the style of OCR

Study the four sources on the Poor Law, and then answer both of the questions.

(a) **Study Sources A and B**
Compare these sources as evidence of reasons for the introduction of the new Poor Law. (20 marks)

(b) **Study all the sources**
Using all these sources *and* your own knowledge, assess the view that 'in order to force the able-bodied to work, the new Poor Law penalised the very people who were in greatest need of relief'. (40 marks)

Source A

Adapted from: Poor Law Report of 1834, commenting on the old Poor Law.

What motive to work has the man who is to receive 10 shillings (50p) every Saturday, not because 10 shillings is the value of his week's labour, but because his family consists of five persons? What motive has the man who knows that his income will be increased by nothing but by an increase of his family, and diminished by nothing but by a decrease in size of his family, that it has no reference to his skill, honesty, or his diligence – what motive has he to acquire or to preserve any of these merits?

Source B

From: a report from Market Harborough, a new Poor Law union in Leicestershire, on the implementation of the New Poor Law (Second Annual Report of the Poor Law Commission, 1836).

People who never could be made to work have become good labourers, and do not express any dissatisfaction with the measure. In most parishes the moral character of the poor is improving: there is a readiness to be more orderly and well-behaved. The great body of the labouring poor have become reconciled [used] to it; the workhouse is held in great dread.

Source C

From: RG Gammage, History of the Chartist Movement, *1854. Gammage was a working man, later to be a Chartist leader in his home town of Northampton and here he reflects on the effects of the new Poor Law on the working classes.*

Huge, prison-like workhouses had risen serving to remind the poor of their coming doom. With scanty wages, in many instances insufficient to support life in a tolerable state of comfort, there was nothing before them but misery in the present, and the Bastille* in the future, in which they were to be immured [imprisoned] when the rich oppressor no longer required their services.

[*The prison in Paris, liberated in the French Revolution, which was seen as a symbol of oppression.]

Source D

Adapted from: Derek Fraser, The Evolution of the British Welfare State, *1973. Fraser, a historian, comments on the difficulty of implementing the new Poor Law.*

By imposing the principles of the 1834 Report on the Poor Law, Parliament provided officials, both local and national, with the impossible task of combining deterrence and humane relief within the same system.

Exam tips

The cross-references are intended to take you straight to the material that will help you to answer the questions.

(a) For question **(a)** it is best to compare the two sources in parallel, i.e. to identify and analyse similarities and differences in both together, rather than examine one of them first and then the other.

- Identify what they tell us, directly or indirectly, about motives for introducing the new law.
- Source A contains recommendations for the new law whereas B is commenting on its impact.
- Does this make Source A more useful or reliable than B for analysing motives for introducing the new law? Can B be of any use at all?

- Compare the provenance [origins] of the two sources (e.g. who produced them and why?) and whether this makes any difference to the uses a historian might make of them as evidence.

(b) You have to write an essay for question **(b)**. That means constructing an answer, with arguments both to support and to refute the statement. In doing this, you should use evidence from the sources, quoting phrases rather than whole sentences, as well as your wider knowledge. The strongest answers will group the sources, as shown below. Arguments to support the statement come from all the sources:

- Sources A and B both have evidence from which we can infer that the new law was intended to force the able-bodied to work. Make reference to particular phrases.
- Source C suggests that people who had 'scanty wages', when in work, might be put in prison-like conditions when their 'oppressor no longer required their services', suggesting that they were penalised when most needy, while D supports both parts of the statement in referring to two conflicting purposes of the Act.

   Arguments which disagree that the needy were penalised can be taken from sources A and B:

- Source A from which we can deduce that the new law was designed to encourage 'skill, honesty' and 'diligence'.
- Source B – people 'have become good labourers', 'moral character is improving' while admitting that the 'workhouse is held in dread' which can be interpreted both to refute and to support the statement. But how impartial is Source B and how typical is Market Harborough?
- Make critical comment about possible bias, e.g. in A, B and C.

   Use your wider knowledge to illustrate areas where things were not so black and white, e.g.

- the more humane, outdoor relief continued to be main form of relief while recognising that for those inside the workhouse, even those 'in greatest need of relief', conditions were harsh
- in practice, a certain amount of autonomy remained with the local Poor Law authorities to determine how relief was administered, e.g. some of the most needy were probably better provided for inside than they would have been outside the workhouse even if there were also instances of great inhumanity (e.g. at Andover)
- did some parts of the country fit some parts of the statement better? Was there an industrial/rural or north/south England divide?

   Conclude with your overall judgement about why, and to what extent, both you and the sources agree with the statement.

7

Chartism: The Working-class Challenge

POINTS TO CONSIDER

In the years following the Reform Act of 1832, the laws passed by the reformed Parliament and actions taken by the Whig government led to the emergence of Chartism. The rise and development of this popular, mass movement is examined through the themes of:

- The origins of Chartism
- The Charter, the Petition and the Convention 1837–9
- Chartism in the 1840s

Key dates

1832		Reform Act passed
1834	February	Grand National Consolidated Trade Union was launched
	March	Tolpuddle Martyrs sentenced to transportation
1835		Municipal Corporations Act excluded working classes from local government
1836		Taxes on newspapers lowered
1837		*Northern Star* newspaper started in Leeds by Feargus O'Connor
1837–8		Anti-Poor Law campaign
1838	May	Publication of the 'People's Charter'
	Aug–Oct	Mass meetings elected delegates to Chartist Convention
1839	July	First Chartist petition rejected by Parliament
		Birmingham riots
	September	Chartist Convention broke up
	November	Newport Rising
1840		National Charter Association set up
1842	May	Second Chartist petition rejected by Parliament
	August	'Plug' strikes and riots
1845		Chartist Land Plan started
1848	April	Chartist meeting on Kennington Common, London
		Third Chartist petition rejected by Parliament

1 | The Origins of Chartism

Key question
Why did the working classes feel let down by the Reform Act?

In 1831–2 hundreds of thousands of working people had marched and demonstrated in support of the Reform Bill. Although it did not give the vote to working people, many of them were swept along in their enthusiasm for the Bill, confident in the hope that it would be a first step on the road to democracy. They joined the middle classes – the manufacturers and the shopkeepers – in what was a national campaign for reform. Many working people first became involved in politics at this time. Many of them had their first experience of attending a political meeting, reading a radical pamphlet or joining a political club.

There were other reasons for hope as well. The passing of the Bill seemed to show that a well-organised campaign, with demonstrations, meetings, pamphlets and newspapers, all backed up by huge numbers, *could* achieve change in Parliament.

Not surprisingly, however, working people were disappointed when they understood what the terms of the Reform Act really meant in practice. The first Reform Parliament looked and behaved very much like those before reform. In composition, the new Parliament looked even less sympathetic to the working classes. Henry Hunt, long-time champion of universal suffrage, lost his seat in Parliament. So too did Michael Sadler, who had tried to pass a bill for factory reform in Parliament: instead of electing Sadler as their MP, the newly-enfranchised middle classes of Leeds used their votes to elect a local factory owner. In the years following the passing of the Reform Act of 1832, the working classes felt increasingly betrayed by the middle classes and the actions of the new Parliament seemed to demonstrate even more opposition to the interests of the working classes than the unreformed Parliaments had done.

We will now examine the sequence of events that turned working-class disappointment to anger and that led to the emergence of a new, national, political campaign known as Chartism.

The Factory Act 1833

This Act was a huge disappointment to the reformers who had campaigned for the Ten Hour Day (see page 97). All they got out of Parliament were restrictions on the hours that children could work in factories. Men and women would still have to work long hours. The new Parliament showed little interest in the improvement of working conditions. The Ten Hour Movement and its Short Time Committees continued to campaign for factory reform.

The attack on trade unions 1834

Key question
How did the Whig government respond to the growth of trade unionism?

Trade unions had been legalised with the repeal of the Combination Acts in 1824 (see page 39). Unions began to be organised in many workshops and factories. When trade improved, between 1833 and 1835, unions were in a stronger position to bargain for better pay and conditions. There were a

Key dates

Grand National Consolidated Trade Union launched: February 1834

Tolpuddle Martyrs sentenced to transportation: March 1834

Municipal Corporations Act excluded working classes from local government: 1835

Taxes on newspapers lowered: 1836

number of small strikes but what worried the government more was the development of large, general unions that united workers from many different trades into big, permanent organisations. This concern turned to alarm when, in February 1834, the Grand National Consolidated Trade Union (GNCTU) was launched. This was to be a national organisation of workers, skilled and unskilled, from all trades. It promised to be huge.

In fact, it never attracted more than 16,000 members and was poorly organised, but the Whig government saw it as a threat. In March 1834 six farm labourers from the village of Tolpuddle, in Dorset, were arrested for taking illegal oaths (making secret promises) when joining a trade union. This was illegal under an old law. They were put on trial and sentenced to seven years' transportation. The judge said the sentence was 'an example and a warning'. The GNCTU took up the case of the Tolpuddle Martyrs and held a protest rally in London, but the Whig government refused to change the sentence. They seemed determined to smother the growth of trade unionism. This policy and a decline in trade from 1836 led to a drop in trade union membership.

The Municipal Corporations Act 1835

This Act (see page 101) extended the vote for local town councils to all ratepayers. This effectively excluded the working classes from participating in local government because, to be a ratepayer, you had to own property and very few of the working classes did so. As with parliamentary reform in 1832, the working classes were being shut out of the political process. Furthermore, the new town councils began to establish modern police forces that many of the working classes saw as threatening. In Lancashire, local workers referred to the police as the 'plague of blue locusts'.

Key question
What impact did the unstamped press have on the radical movement?

The 'war of the unstamped' press

Since the so-called Gagging Acts of 1819 (see page 25), newspapers had had to pay a government stamp duty. This was an attempt to deprive the radical press of its working-class readers because the tax meant that papers cost about 3p (equivalent to more than £1 today). However, not all newspapers obeyed the law. The *Poor Man's Guardian* was sold for a penny and sold over 15,000 copies a week. Other papers followed this lead. **Henry Hetherington**, the owner of the *Poor Man's Guardian*, was imprisoned twice but this did not stop the paper from being published in secret locations. In London alone, 740 sellers of unstamped newspapers were put on trial between 1831 and 1836. Eventually the Whig government gave in and, in 1836, lowered the tax to a point where newspapers could be sold for 1.5p. This was an important victory since an active press was vital in developing and spreading radical ideas. Furthermore, it showed that a determined and well-organised campaign could force the government to give way.

Key term

Henry Hetherington
He led the 'war of the unstamped', the campaign against 'taxes on knowledge'.

The Anti-Poor Law campaign 1837–8

Key question
How important was the Anti-Poor Law campaign in the emergence of Chartism?

Key question

Out of all the developments that led to the emergence of Chartism, the campaign launched against the new Poor Law in 1837 was by far the most significant. None of the actions of the reformed Parliament seemed quite so punitive as this new law. To working people, it looked as if it was designed to rob them of what they saw as their 'right' to poor relief by forcing them into the workhouse if they came on hard times. Furthermore, it demonstrated how much control Parliament had over the daily lives of working people and how little control they had over their own lives. Even family life seemed to be under threat with the rule that the sexes should be separated in the workhouse. It was not surprising that women played such an active role in the Anti-Poor Law campaign and in the Chartist movement that followed.

Radicals like Oastler, Fielden (see page 98) and Feargus O'Connor, as well as the Methodist preacher **J.R. Stephens**, began to tour the country, giving speeches, raising funds and setting up local clubs to oppose the introduction of the new Poor Law in the industrial north. The Short Time Committees, which had rallied support for the 10-hour working day, now transferred their energies into this new campaign. O'Connor, who was to become the best known and most powerful Chartist leader, started his *Northern Star* newspaper in Leeds. It played a crucial role in spreading news and views across the country, both in this campaign and in the next 10 years as the leading Chartist newspaper.

J.R. Stephens
A brilliant orator. He attacked the new Poor Law and became a fervent Chartist. He famously said, to a large crowd in Manchester, that universal suffrage was 'a knife and fork question'.

Key term

Northern Star newspaper started in Leeds by Feargus O'Connor: 1837

Key date

When John Fielden proposed the repeal of the new Poor Law in Parliament, the House of Commons voted against it by 309 to 17 votes. It seemed to the working classes that there was no chance of ever getting Parliament to pass laws that would improve the working and living conditions of poor people. While working people produced the wealth of the country, the 'idle' classes, who were represented in Parliament, held on to the power and lived off the fruits of other men's labour. A future Chartist leader wrote:

> It is POWER that the millions must obtain and retain if they would enjoy the produce of their own labour.

Working men would have to enter Parliament itself if they were to secure control over, and improve, their own lives.

Summary diagram: The origins of Chartism

Attack on trade unions 1834
Showed government opposition to development of general unions

Reform Bill campaign 1831–2
Provides a model of successful mass movement and a spur to further campaigning

Factory Act 1833
Showed reformed Parliament to be opposed to factory reform. Ten Hour Movement continued to campaign

Why did Chartism emerge in the 1830s?

Municipal Corporations Act 1835
Excluded working classes from local government

War of the unstamped
Showed pressure could win concessions from government and created the conditions for an active Chartist press

Anti-Poor Law campaign, 1837–8
Confirmed government's hostility to the working classes and their needs. Led to emergence of mass movement and start of *Northern Star* newspaper

2 | The Charter, the Petition and the Convention 1837–9

In 1837 six members of the London Working Men's Association (LWMA), assisted by six Radical MPs, drew up a list of six points for political reform. These six points became the basis of the 'People's Charter' which was published in May 1838. This document was to give its name to the movement known as Chartism.

The Six Points

- **Universal manhood suffrage**: all men over 21 years of age would be allowed to vote
- **Vote by secret ballot**: so that all votes could be cast without fear of pressure from landlords or employers
- **Annual Parliaments**: general elections to take place every year
- **Equal electoral districts**: so that all constituencies contained roughly the same number of electors
- **Abolition of the property qualification for MPs**: so that someone standing for Parliament no longer had to own property
- **Payment for MPs**: so that working men could afford to give up their jobs and become MPs

None of these points was new. Radicals had been calling for all of these changes for many years. What was new was that these six political demands became the symbol and the focus of what was to be a national mass movement. Chartism attracted the support of hundreds of thousands of working people for over 10 years. It

Key date
Publication of the 'People's Charter': May 1838

was the nearest thing Britain has had to a national rising in
modern times.

The National Petition and the Chartist Convention

The Charter containing the six points was taken up by the
Birmingham Political Union (see page 66), now revived by its
leader, Thomas Attwood, and by northern activists like John
Fielden and Feargus O'Connor who had been campaigning
against the Poor Law. It was adopted by radicals right across the
country. It was then launched in Glasgow, where several textile
workers had been imprisoned for leading a strike in May 1838.
Here it was decided that a petition, demanding the six points of
the Charter, would be presented to Parliament. Again, this was
nothing new. This petition, however, was going to be different. It
was going to collect so many signatures that Parliament would not
be able to ignore it. Those signatures would be collected at mass
meetings held all over the country. Also at these meetings
delegates would be appointed to attend a National Convention
which would in turn organise the presentation of this National
Petition to Parliament.

All went according to plan. Huge meetings were held: over
200,000 people attended each of the meetings in Birmingham,
Manchester and Leeds. Smaller meetings were held in hundreds of
other towns across the country. These were organised and
publicised with the help of the Chartist press, among which the
Northern Star was the most important. By 1839 it was selling 50,000
copies a week, similar in circulation to *The Times*, the most famous
national newspaper. At these meetings, signatures were collected
and delegates elected to the National Convention that met in
London in February 1839. The Convention claimed to represent
all the people, unlike Parliament. It was a kind of 'anti-Parliament'
or, as some Chartists preferred, the 'real' Parliament. Over one and
a quarter million signatures were collected in support of the
petition. Both the size of the petition (it was three miles long) and
the level of national co-ordination were unprecedented. Yet, in July
1839, Parliament rejected the petition by 235 votes to 46. Most
MPs simply decided to have nothing to do with it.

'Moral force' versus 'physical force'

From now onwards, things did not go according to plan because
there was no plan. The members of the Convention had discussed
what to do if Parliament rejected the petition but had not been
able to reach a decision. The big issue was whether or not to use
force.

Most Chartists were passionate believers in moral force. They
believed that Chartism was so obviously a just and fair cause that
they could win people over with the power of their arguments.
However, most also believed that they needed the sheer force of
numbers behind them if they were to persuade a property-owning
Parliament to agree to universal suffrage. Many of the meetings
held before the Chartist Convention had used 'the language of

Key question
What was the
significance of the
National Petition?

Key dates
Launch of the Charter
in Glasgow: May 1838

Mass meetings
elected delegates to
Chartist Convention:
August–October 1838

National Convention
met in London:
February 1839

First Chartist petition
rejected by
Parliament: July 1839

Key question
How did members of
the Convention view
the use of force?

A Chartist demonstration.

menace', just as they had in the Reform Bill campaign of 1831–2. At the big Birmingham meeting in May, Attwood had said:

> No blood shall be shed by us; but if our enemies shed blood – if they attack the people – they must take the consequences upon their own heads.

This idea of 'defensive violence' was adopted by many Chartist leaders. It was summed up by the slogan 'Peacefully if we can, forcefully if we must'. There was not a clear-cut division between 'moral force' and 'physical force' Chartists. O'Connor has often been associated with 'physical force' Chartism, yet he was primarily an advocate of the peaceful approach. He knew that working men could not defeat the soldiers of the regular army.

In the Convention it was suggested that a **Sacred Month** (or a national holiday) should be adopted if Parliament rejected the petition. This meant that Chartists would withdraw their labour and go on strike for a month. The delegates at the Convention recognised that this would be a direct challenge to the employers and to the governing classes as a whole, especially as it had the potential to wreck the economy. It would probably bring about a physical confrontation in which troops would be used and many people killed. Although the Convention decided, in the end, not to recommend a Sacred Month, discussions like these scared several of the Chartist delegates, especially the middle-class ones. Attwood, himself an employer, left the Convention in September 1839 saying that he 'washed his hands of any idea, of any appeal to physical force'. Yet he himself had used the 'language of menace' a year before.

In July 1839, members of the (London) Metropolitan Police were used to break up a peaceful Chartist meeting in Birmingham. It led to a fortnight of rioting. **William Lovett**, who was Secretary of the Chartist Convention, produced a placard

Key terms

Sacred Month
The proposal for a month-long strike if the National Petition was rejected.

William Lovett
One of the chief authors of the People's Charter. Like many other Chartists, he was imprisoned for a time. After his release in 1840, Lovett devoted his time to the improvement of working-class education and was much criticised by O'Connor for relying purely on 'moral force' Chartism.

accusing the local authorities in Birmingham of 'a flagrant and unjust outrage, using a bloody and unconstitutional force from London' to break up the meeting. For this, he was arrested and sentenced to a year in prison. His crime was **seditious libel**. Lovett is usually seen as a leading 'moral force' Chartist, yet here he was defending the actions of the Birmingham crowd in fighting the police. He would have regarded this as an example of 'defensive violence'.

Birmingham riots: July 1839

Key date

Seditious libel Use of language encouraging rebellion against the State.

Key term

The Convention breaks up, September 1839

Although the Convention voted against the idea of a month-long strike, the delegates called for a three-day strike in August. The response in the localities varied: many Chartists refused to leave work and so lose their pay (and, perhaps, their jobs) for what they saw as a short-term gesture. Others, in the most loyal Chartist districts, stayed off work and attended rallies. Many local leaders were arrested for their speeches, for threatening behaviour or for riot.

The Chartist Convention broke up in September 1839. There was still much support for direct action, despite the arrest of many leading Chartists, but the rejection of the petition had led to confusion about what to do next. The Convention delegates returned to their localities and the movement lost its central direction. Much would now depend on local leaders.

Chartist Convention broke up: September 1839

Key date

Key debate

Was Chartism a political or an economic movement?

In 1839, the writer Thomas Carlyle described Chartism as 'bitter discontent grown fierce and mad'. Historians have debated whether this discontent was caused by political or economic factors. It is certainly true that years of maximum support for Chartism were years of economic depression (1838–9, 1842 and 1848) when trade was poor and many were thrown out of work. This has led some historians to see Chartism as a form of 'hunger politics'.

However, other historians have concluded that it was politically motivated. They stress that Chartism grew out of the anger and frustration that working people felt in the years after the Reform Act. Parliament showed little interest in the living and working conditions of ordinary people, therefore working people would have to enter Parliament themselves and make the reforms that would improve their lives. The six points of the Charter would enable them to do this. Whatever the local conditions, working people throughout Britain could agree on the political points of the Charter. It was the one thing that united all those who met, marched and demonstrated. It kept alive working-class hopes throughout the years 1838–48.

Chartism was certainly fuelled by unemployment, low wages and hunger but the Charter was seen as the solution. If working people were to take control of their own lives and bring about social and economic change, they would have to gain political power first. Chartism is best seen as both an economic *and* a political movement in that it was composed of political activists who wanted to use politics to improve their living and working conditions and thus make for a more just and fair society.

The Newport Rising 1839

Key question
Was the Newport Rising an attempt to overthrow the government or a demonstration that went wrong?

Key date

Newport Rising: November 1839

In November 1839 nearly 10,000 men marched from towns and villages in South Wales to Newport in Monmouthshire. Most of them were miners and iron workers. Many of them were armed – with pikes, guns or just wooden clubs – and they marched in military formation. They arrived at dawn on 4 November in Newport. They surrounded the Westgate Hotel where some local Chartist leaders were held under armed guard. There was a small force of troops who started firing and, after the Chartists had fled, over 20 bodies were left at the scene. It is uncertain who fired first or what the intentions of the marchers were.

One historian believes that a 'monster demonstration' had been intended, a show of force to protest against the recent arrest of local Chartists. But the authorities saw it as an armed uprising intended as the signal for similar risings elsewhere. It had certainly been planned for some time and kept secret from the authorities. One Chartist, a 17-year-old boy, left a letter to his parents before setting off:

> I shall this night be engaged in a struggle for freedom and should it please God to spare my life I shall see you soon; but if not, grieve not for me for I shall fall in a noble cause.

The historical evidence suggests that the rising was not part of a co-ordinated, national plot, but that the plan was to take control of the town of Newport and to inspire Chartists elsewhere to do the same. Three of the leaders were sentenced to death for attempting to overthrow the State by force, but the Whig government, keen to avoid making martyrs, changed the sentence to transportation instead. The rising did, however, give the government the justification it needed to move against the Chartists and, over the next two years, nearly 500 were imprisoned.

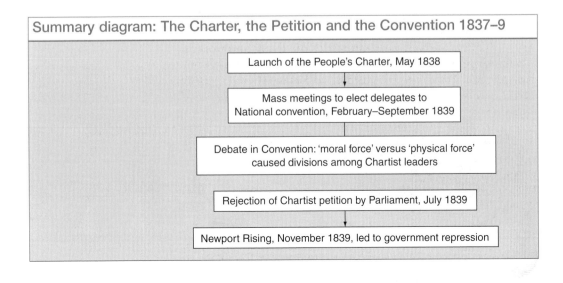

Summary diagram: The Charter, the Petition and the Convention 1837–9

Launch of the People's Charter, May 1838

Mass meetings to elect delegates to National convention, February–September 1839

Debate in Convention: 'moral force' versus 'physical force' caused divisions among Chartist leaders

Rejection of Chartist petition by Parliament, July 1839

Newport Rising, November 1839, led to government repression

3 | Chartism in the 1840s

The National Charter Association

Key question
What new strategies emerged after 1839?

Despite the failure of the first petition and the arrest of hundreds of Chartist leaders, the Chartist movement did not collapse, but it had to be reorganised. Most Chartists recognised that a stronger central organisation was necessary to prevent the movement fragmenting. While O'Connor was imprisoned in York Castle, he continued to write articles for the *Northern Star*. Among other things, he encouraged the establishment of the **National Charter Association** (NCA). Set up in 1840, this was to be the most important Chartist organisation for the rest of the decade. By 1842, it had 50,000 members in 400 branches across the country.

National Charter Association formed: 1840

'New moves'

Meanwhile, other Chartist leaders embarked on different strategies. When William Lovett was released from prison in 1840, he concentrated his energies on promoting education for the working classes. He devised a scheme with schools, libraries and teacher training colleges. He and several other Chartist leaders argued that the working classes had to prove, by self-help and self-improvement, that they were responsible citizens. Respectable behaviour would calm the fears of the propertied classes and show that the working classes were 'ready' for the vote. Other Chartists advocated teetotal Chartism (i.e. taking the vow not to drink alcohol), and, in Birmingham, a Chartist Church was set up.

National Charter Association
The NCA was a national, political organisation. It set up branches across Britain and members paid subscriptions to join. Many historians see it as the first independent, working-class political party, a forerunner of the Labour Party.

These new schemes were all exclusively 'moral force' strategies. O'Connor, however, attacked these 'new moves', not because he disapproved of education, teetotalism or Christianity, but because he saw them as distracting attention from the strategy of petitioning backed up by weight of numbers.

O'Connor and his supporters, who were the majority of Chartists, organised the collection of signatures for a second petition and the meeting of another convention in 1842. Three million signatures were collected for the petition. Helped by

The second Chartist petition is carried to the House of Commons, 1842.

Key date

Second Chartist petition rejected by Parliament: May 1842

economic depression and rising unemployment, 1842 was probably the year of Chartism's greatest strength in terms of mass support. But, yet again, in May 1842, Parliament rejected the petition by a huge majority.

The 'Plug' strikes and riots, August 1842

Key question

How did the government react to the Plug disturbances?

A few months later, and much to the surprise of many Chartist leaders, a rash of strikes broke out in August 1842. With many workers being laid off and even more suffering wage cuts, strikes spread from Lancashire and Yorkshire to the industrial parts of the Midlands and Scotland. As the strikers went from factory to factory gaining support, they pulled the plugs from the boilers, thus forcing the factories to close down.

There were many violent confrontations between strikers and the authorities. Local police forces were used effectively and troops were moved quickly around the trouble spots using the recently built railways. Hundreds of arrests were made, this time on orders of the new Conservative government that had been elected in 1841. The new government was swifter and firmer in its response to Chartist disturbances than the Whigs had been. By the end of 1842, about 1500 people had been put on trial for Chartist-related offences.

Plug riots in Preston, Lancashire, in August 1842.

Economic recovery and the Land Plan 1845–8

Key question

What was the Chartist Land Plan?

Chartism lost its mass support in the mid-1840s. This was for several reasons:

- the arrest of many of its leaders
- divisions among other leaders
- economic recovery, especially with the boom in railway building
- reforms carried out by Peel's government.

The reforms of Peel's Conservative government are explained fully in Chapter 8. In brief, they showed that even a Parliament in which the poor had no say was capable of recognising and

Profile: Feargus O'Connor 1794–1855

1794 – Born into an Irish landowning family
1832 – Elected MP for County Cork in Ireland
1837 – Established the *Northern Star* newspaper
1840 – Found guilty of publishing seditious libel (language
        encouraging rebellion against the government) and
        imprisoned for 18 months
1845 – Set up the Chartist Land Plan (see below)
1847 – MP for Nottingham, the only Chartist elected to
        Parliament in the general election.
1855 – Died

O'Connor trained as a lawyer and came to prominence when he established the *Northern Star* in Leeds in 1837. He campaigned against the new Poor Law and later emerged as the most powerful and controversial Chartist leader.

The *Northern Star* was the most widely read Chartist journal; its weekly delivery was awaited eagerly in towns and villages across Britain. O'Connor wrote the front page 'letter' each week, but many others contributed. The paper acted as a unifying element, enabling news and views to be exchanged. It also helped to sustain Chartism as a national movement at times when it might have fragmented into a collection of local campaigns. O'Connor appointed and paid agents to work in different parts of the country so that they could report for the paper and also act as full-time organisers. Profits from the paper were used to pay the expenses of Chartists who were put on trial and to support the families of those imprisoned.

O'Connor was a powerful speaker, but was widely accused of being arrogant and a 'rabble rouser'. Lovett and other 'moral force' leaders criticised the violence of his language and some said that he raised unrealistic expectations in his listeners. But he was praised by many of those who worked closely with him. The historian Dorothy Thompson has written:

No other leader or would-be leader in those years had the energy, ability or charisma of Feargus O'Connor. For good or ill, he was the main inspiration and guiding force of the movement.

O'Connor died, insane, in 1855: 20,000 people attended his funeral.

responding to distress in industrial areas and passing reforms. These reforms took some of the sting out of Chartism.

Nevertheless, Chartist hopes were kept alive, even revived, by the Chartist Land Company. This was O'Connor's scheme to establish rural Chartist communities. Chartists were invited to buy shares in the company; if their names were drawn out by lot, they would receive plots of land to cultivate. Among the industrial working class this proved to be hugely popular. By 1848, 100,000

Chartist Land Plan
started: 1845

Key date

people had subscribed and five communities had been set up, each with homes, schools and parks.

However, the authorities hounded O'Connor and his company. They failed to discover any evidence of financial malpractice, but they did find a legal technicality that enabled them to wind up the company.

1848: the final phase

Key question
What happened in 1848?

In the 1847 general election O'Connor was elected to Parliament, the only Chartist to succeed in doing so. Inspired by this and news of another revolution in France, a third Chartist petition and convention was planned for April 1848.

Support for Chartism again increased, partly because of the return of economic depression and the resulting distress that was experienced in the industrial areas. A mass meeting was planned to take place on Kennington Common, just south of the Houses of Parliament, where the petition would be delivered after the meeting.

Key date

Third Chartist petition and meeting in London: April 1848

The government was not taking any chances. They had 7000 troops, 4000 policemen and 85,000 special constables recruited, mostly from the middle class. In the event the meeting attracted a crowd of only about 20,000. It went off peacefully and the procession was stopped before it reached Parliament. However, the leaders and the petition, with five million signatures, were allowed through. A parliamentary committee examined the petition and declared that less than half the signatures were genuine. Again, it was rejected.

There was an upsurge of violence in the Chartist heartlands of Lancashire and Yorkshire, particularly in the most depressed textile-producing areas, and there were many more arrests. However, after 1848, support for Chartism declined rapidly. Chartists continued to meet and hold conventions through the 1850s but there was no longer a mass following.

Did Chartism fail?

Key question
What did Chartism achieve?

None of the Six Points of the Charter was achieved until the twentieth century (and one, annual parliaments, has never been accepted). To that extent, Chartism was a failure. The governing classes were never going to give way. They had brought the middle classes into the political process in 1832 and, after that, the property-owning classes as a whole were united in their determination to exclude the working classes.

Not surprisingly, the power of the State was too strong for the Chartists. The army was loyal and professional police forces had been established across most of the country by the 1840s. The government had the support of the magistrates and extensive use was made of the courts to pick off and imprison Chartist leaders. The railways enabled troops to be moved far more quickly to where they were needed and the government made good use of another new technology – the electric telegraph – to speed up communications.

But there were positive outcomes for the Chartists. Hundreds of thousands of working men and women – there were over 100 female radical associations in the 1840s – gained valuable political experience. The working classes had become far more independent and resourceful. In the years ahead, working people:

- set up trade unions and **Friendly Societies**
- continued to be engaged in political clubs and societies
- and, at the end of the century, helped to establish the Labour Party, set up to represent the working classes in Parliament.

Chartism had provided an invaluable education in politics.

Friendly Societies Organisations to which members made a small weekly contribution and were provided with support in sickness or old age.

Key term

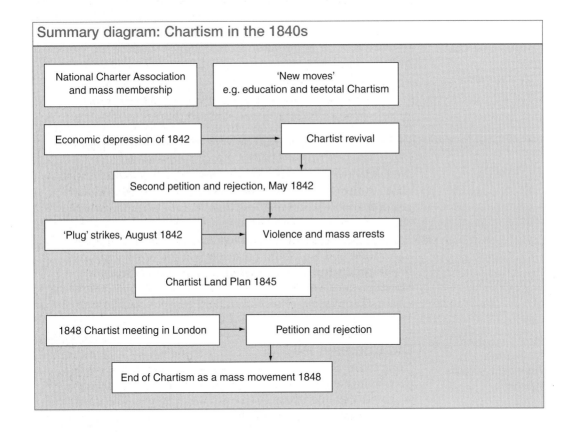

Summary diagram: Chartism in the 1840s

- National Charter Association and mass membership
- 'New moves' e.g. education and teetotal Chartism
- Economic depression of 1842 → Chartist revival
- Second petition and rejection, May 1842
- 'Plug' strikes, August 1842 → Violence and mass arrests
- Chartist Land Plan 1845
- 1848 Chartist meeting in London → Petition and rejection
- End of Chartism as a mass movement 1848

Study Guide: AS Questions

In the style of AQA

Read the following source and then answer the questions that follow.

From: The Nature of Chartism in Britain, 1815–1867, *by Hugh Cunningham, 1994.*

In so far as it was a political movement, Chartism was seen as a product of the disenchantment between the working classes and the Whig government after 1832.

(a) Comment on Chartism 'as a political movement' in the context of the late 1830s. (3 marks)
(b) Explain why Chartism attracted mass support in the years leading up to 1841. (7 marks)
(c) Explain the importance of economic and social discontent, in relation to other factors, in leading to the defeat of the Whigs in 1841. (15 marks)

Exam tips

The cross-references are intended to take you straight to the material that will help you to answer the questions.

(a) With question (a) only a few lines are required for 3 marks so you should:

- summarise the political aims of the Chartists with reference to the six points of the Charter, but you do not need to provide a long list of the points
- show how these formed the political core of the movement in the late 1830s even if it was economic discontent that brought the mass support (see page 118).

(b) In question (b) you will need to explain both the political and economic factors. It would be a good idea to start with the political factors, especially the reasons for 'the disenchantment between the working classes and the Whig government after 1832' referred to in the source. These are covered on pages 112–14. These factors are likely to include:

- disappointment with the 1832 Reform Act (and later local government reform) and the 1833 Factory Act
- the anger and the organised opposition provoked by the 1834 new Poor Law
- the government attitude towards trade unionism and the radical press.

    Although Chartism arose from a well-established radical tradition (think back to the years after 1815), it was the economic depression that produced mass discontent which in turn brought mass support for Chartism. You will need to explain this, giving examples of mass support, e.g. at meetings (see page 116).

(c) For question (c) you will need to re-read Chapter 6, especially the section on the decline of the Whigs (pages 103–6). However, much of the material for your essay will come from this chapter In your introduction, you should identify key areas that you will examine. This will include:

- the economic and social discontent associated with Chartism
- sources of political discontent such as (i) the Whigs' reliance on Radical and Irish votes in Parliament and (ii) the fears, voiced by Tories in the 1841 election, about threats to the Church of England and the Corn Laws.

    These issues will need to be explained and assessed for *their importance in leading to the Whigs' defeat.* You will need to explore the role of Peel and the Tories in exploiting and highlighting Whig weaknesses (e.g. in dealing with the Chartist threat). Do not overlook the fact that it is only the propertied classes who voted the Whigs out of power. So discontent caused by the new Poor Law may not, in itself, be a major factor because it is the disenfranchised, the non-voters, who suffer the most. However, the disturbances that result, especially in the north of England, may make the Whigs look weak on law and order to the property-owning voters. In conclusion, you should state what you believe to be the key factors leading to the defeat of the Whigs and, specifically, identify the importance of economic and social discontent.

In the style of Edexcel

Answer both parts of the question.

(a) Why did the working classes support the 1832 Reform Act?

(20 marks)

(b) How far do you agree that the origins of Chartism are to be found in the 1832 Reform Act? (40 marks)

Exam tips

The cross-references are intended to take you straight to the material that will help you to answer the questions.

(a) For question **(a)**, re-read page 80 of Chapter 6. The key thing to note at the start is that very few of the working classes were enfranchised by the Act yet most supported it at the time. Key points to explain will be:

- the Act won wide support because it was a bold move and it swept away many small, corrupt pocket boroughs
- many people were carried away by the excitement of the agitation and of the 1831 election campaign
- a Whig Reform Bill was preferable to a Tory government under Wellington
- the Act might be a first instalment of reform, with universal suffrage to come later.

You might also add:

- the hope of some of the working classes that the newly enfranchised middle classes might be more sympathetic to working-class demands than the aristocratic, landowning classes had been
- it was a major reform where little more than tinkering had been carried out before so there was great optimism about further change to come.

(b) Question **(b)** is a 40-mark question that requires an essay in which you will need to (i) examine what origins Chartism had in the Reform Act, (ii) examine other factors that gave rise to Chartism and (iii) make a balanced judgement about which were more important. Read pages 112–14 again. For the origins, you should discuss:

- how the hopes and expectations of the working classes, who made up the majority of Chartists, were raised by the Act
- how a national, well-organised Reform campaign with mass support was *seen* to have secured the passing of the Act and this set an example to the working classes
- how disappointment with the results of the Act turned to anger and discontent and thus fed into Chartism.

You should then discuss the actions of the government and reformed Parliament after 1832, showing how these intensified working-class determination to achieve political power through the six points of the Charter. You might mention:

- 1833 Factory Act and Short Time Committees
- government attitude to Trade Unions
- local government reform
- government repression of the press and the 'war of the unstamped'
- the campaign against the new Poor Law

Think: to what extent were the laws passed after 1832 those of a reformed Parliament? Or would a pre-1832 Parliament have passed similar laws? Other points to consider are:

- the importance of radical agitation before 1832, particularly from 1815 to 1819, in developing working-class consciousness/feeling and political organisation/methods, e.g. mass meetings, radical press
- how important were economic factors, e.g. the depression of 1837–8?

In conclusion, you need to weigh up what you think are the key points in order to make your final judgement about *the extent* to which the 1832 Act gave rise to Chartism.

In the style of OCR

Study the four sources on the nature of Chartism below, and then answer both of the questions.

(a) Study Sources A and B
Compare these sources as evidence for the motives of the Chartists. (20 marks)

(b) Study all the sources
Using *all* these sources *and* your own knowledge, assess the view that: 'Chartism was a protest against physical suffering and universal suffrage was thought to be its remedy'. (40 marks)

Source A

From: Bronterre O'Brien, writing in The Operative, *17 March 1839. O'Brien, a leading Chartist, was a journalist and thinker whom O'Connor called 'the Schoolmaster of Chartism'. He was editor of* The Operative.

Universal suffrage means meat and drink and clothing, good hours, and good beds, and good substantial furniture for every man, woman and child who will do a fair day's work. Universal suffrage means a complete mastery, by all the people over all the laws and institutions in the country; and with that mastery the power of providing suitable employment for all, as well as of securing to all the full proceeds of their employment.

Source B

From: B. Wilson, The Struggles of an Old Chartist, *1887. Here Wilson, a Chartist, recalls the days of the Chartist movement.*

I have never known a case of plunder in the town, though thousands of Chartists have marched through its streets to meetings in various places. What they wanted was a voice in making the laws they were called upon to obey; they believed that taxation without representation was tyranny, and ought to be resisted; they took a leading part in agitating in favour of the ten hours question; the repeal of the taxes on knowledge, education and the land question, for they were the true pioneers in all the great movements of their time.

Source C

From: Harriet Martineau, History of England during the Thirty Years Peace, *1849. Here Martineau, a middle-class writer, examines the reasons for the growth of Chartism.*

What was it all about? Those who have not looked into Chartism think that it was one thing – a revolution. Those who look deeper – who go out onto the moors by torchlight, who talk with a suffering brother under the hedge, or beside the loom, who listen to the groups outside the Union workhouse, or in the public house among the Durham coal-pits – will feel long bewildered as to what Chartism is. They will conclude at last that it is another name for popular discontent – a comprehensive general term under which are included all protests against social suffering.

Source D

Adapted from: Archibald Alison, 'The Chartists and Universal Suffrage', in Blackwood's Edinburgh Magazine, *September 1839. This was a Tory journal that was highly critical of the Chartists.*

The working-classes have now proved themselves unworthy of that extension of the Suffrage for which they contend. It is now established beyond all doubt, that Universal Suffrage in reality means nothing else but universal plunder. What the working-classes understand by political power, is just the means of putting their hands in their neighbour's pockets. The belief that the Reform Bill would give them that power, which was the main cause of their support for the Bill, and the disgust at the failure of these hopes, is the principal reason for the present clamour for an extension of the Suffrage.

Exam tips

The cross-references are intended to take you straight to the material that will help you to answer the questions.

(a) For question **(a)** it is best to compare the two sources together, rather than examine one of them first and then the other.

- To *compare* the two sources, you should examine similarities and differences, making use of short quotations (i.e. short phrases rather than whole sentences) from the sources.
- Also, you need to **explain** the similarities and differences, especially as you are being asked to compare them **as evidence**.
  Points to make are:
- O'Brien refers to universal suffrage, not Chartism as such, but universal suffrage is the key point in the Charter. Both refer to the Chartist aim of securing control over the laws passed although O'Brien refers to 'mastery' and Wilson just to 'a voice in making' them.
- O'Brien stresses material/economic needs ('meat and drink and clothing') whereas Wilson goes on to refer to wider social and political goals such as factory reform, 'repeal of taxes on knowledge, education', etc.
- Might the differences be explained by who they were writing for and when? Would this make one more useful or reliable as evidence than the other?

(b) Question **(b)** requires a mini-essay. Rather than deal with each source separately, you should try to group the sources, e.g.

- Sources A and C both agree with this view. They refer to (or imply) economic hardship and physical suffering as the cause of Chartism (lack of food and pay in A and suffering and 'the Union workhouse' in C).
- Sources A and B agree that Chartists want a say in making laws (and, to do this, will need the suffrage).
- By contrast, source D sees plunder as central to Chartism although source B denies that it meant plunder.

As you write, you should make critical comment about the value of the sources, e.g.

- Source D being from a Tory journal is, not surprisingly, damning. Is that out of ignorance of what living and working conditions were like? Or out of fear of the working classes?
- Might source B, written years later by an old Chartist, be keen to defend the Chartist record and make it sound more high-minded (e.g. with mention of education)?
- Perhaps O'Brien (source A) was more representative of what motivated the hungry masses? He certainly sees universal suffrage as the remedy for suffering, as it would mean 'providing suitable employment' and the 'full proceeds ...'.

   Your wider knowledge will undoubtedly inform your answer, especially in explaining the context (e.g. source D from a Tory journal). You should also use your wider knowledge to put the main issues in context, e.g. mass support for Chartism came in times of greatest hunger and suffering, but the movement was sustained for over 10 years by the Charter and its central demand which was for universal suffrage. This, in turn, would relieve suffering and provide for decent living and working conditions. In conclusion, you should make a judgement about how far you, and the sources, support the statement.

8 Reform of the Corn Laws

POINTS TO CONSIDER

The Corn Laws were repealed in 1846. This came about partly as the result of campaigning by the Anti-Corn Law League, but it was the decision of the Prime Minister, Sir Robert Peel, to push it through in 1846. The campaign, the decision-making and the effects of repeal are examined in this chapter as:

- The Challenge of the Anti-Corn Law League
- Sir Robert Peel and the Repeal of the Corn Laws
- Reform and mid-Victorian stability

Key dates

1815		Corn Laws were introduced
1828		Corn Laws were modified with a sliding scale introduced
1838		Anti-Corn Law League was founded
1841		Richard Cobden elected to Parliament
1842		Peel re-introduced income tax and cut many tariffs on imports
1843		John Bright elected to Parliament
1845		Irish Famine
1846	June	Repeal of the Corn Laws
1850		Death of Sir Robert Peel
1851		Great Exhibition

1 | The Challenge of the Anti-Corn Law League

At the beginning of our period, in 1815, one issue more than any other generated agitation across the country. The same issue had an equally dramatic impact on British politics near the end of the period covered by this book. That issue was the **Corn Laws**.

The Corn Laws were introduced in 1815, at the end of the war with France, in order to protect British agriculture from imported wheat. The landed classes who dominated Parliament demanded **agricultural protection** in order to protect Britain from a flood of cheap foreign grain that could ruin British agriculture and produce rural unemployment. Their opponents claimed that the laws were passed simply to protect landowners' profits and

Key term

Corn Laws
Tariffs, or import duties, on foreign wheat. In 1815, importing wheat was banned until British wheat reached 80 shillings (£4) a quarter (about 13 kg).

Key date

The Corn Laws were introduced: 1815

income from rents and that they were a blatant piece of 'class legislation'.

In 1828, the laws were modified. A sliding scale was introduced so that the lower the price of British wheat, the higher the duty on foreign imports. But this was only a minor modification. Ten years later, in 1838, the Anti-Corn Law League was formed to campaign for a complete end to the laws.

The Anti-Corn Law League 1838

The Anti-Corn Law League was founded by a group of factory owners in Manchester in 1838. It had one single, simple aim: the total and immediate **repeal** of the Corn Laws. It was no coincidence that it was founded in Manchester and that its key supporters were owners of textile mills. The reason was that Manchester was the centre of the textile industry, the biggest and most important industry in Britain. This industry depended on exporting much of the cloth it produced. Yet it was restricted from doing so, said the League, by the Corn Laws.

The two main arguments of the Anti-Corn Law League were:

- Foreign countries were prevented from exporting their wheat to Britain so they had less money with which to buy British manufactured goods. Also, the governments of foreign countries sometimes retaliated and put up their own tariffs (or import duties) to keep out British goods. However, if those countries *were* able to sell their wheat to Britain, they would be more likely to buy the goods produced by British industry. This would enable British industry to expand and provide more jobs.
- The Corn Laws were responsible for keeping the price of bread artificially high. Bread was the basic food for working-class families and, if cheap wheat could be imported and the price of bread fell, such families would be better off and have more money to spend on manufactured goods.

Aims and methods of the League

The League was dominated by members of the industrial middle classes. They had won a share in power with the passing of the Reform Act of 1832, but Parliament was still dominated by the landed classes. Proposals made in Parliament for reform of the Corn Laws were regularly rejected by the post-Reform Parliament. One of the League leaders wrote in the *Manchester Times*:

> Nothing was to be expected even from a reformed Parliament without such an outward pressure as carried the Reform Bill.

It was this 'outward pressure' that the League aimed to exert. The examples of the political unions during the Reform Bill crisis and the Catholic Association in the 1820s provided models for the League. The League aimed to win mass support and so exert huge pressure on Parliament and the government. They held meetings, raised funds, and produced pamphlets and their own newspaper. They appointed lecturers who used the new railways to travel around the country. They provided independent newspapers with free reports of their own meetings and, if these

Key question
What were the League's main arguments?

Corn Laws modified with a sliding scale introduced: 1828

Key date

Agricultural protection
The policy of protecting British farming from foreign competition.

Repeal
Withdrawal (of laws, in this case).

Key terms

Key question
What impact did the League have?

Free Trade Hall in Manchester. It could hold 9000 people.

were published, they bought up large numbers of the newspapers to distribute. In Manchester, they built a special Free Trade Hall for their big meetings.

Support for the League

The initial impact was limited and the League nearly went bankrupt in 1839. It won much support among industrialists in northern England but the working classes, especially the Chartists, were very suspicious of the League's slogan of 'cheap bread'. They felt that, if cheaper bread were available, factory owners would simply cut wages knowing that their workers would not be forced into starvation.

Nevertheless, the cry of 'cheap bread' had a wide appeal. It gave the League the appearance of campaigning for social justice. It attracted the support of religious groups who saw it as a crusade to end hardship and distress. Prayers were said for 'our daily bread'. Some supporters argued that free trade between nations would bring about greater international understanding and peace.

However, some League members had an ulterior, political motive. They wanted to challenge the domination of the landed classes. Now that industry was so much more important for the economy and society, they argued, so the industrial and commercial middle classes should take control of the government, even overthrow the landowning aristocracy. In 1843, *The Times* reported that the League's aim was:

> not to open the ports, to facilitate commerce, to enrich England, but to ruin our aristocracy, whom Leaguers envy and detest.

League pressure on Parliament

Key question
What were the League's electoral tactics?

In 1841, the League leader, Richard Cobden, convinced other supporters of the need to win a majority in Parliament to ensure repeal. Free traders should be selected to fight elections. Cobden himself was elected as MP for Stockport, a northern textile town, although the 1841 election as a whole was a crushing victory for the Tories and for protectionism (see page 105). Another League leader, John Bright, was elected to Parliament in 1843. He and Cobden made an impact in the House of Commons, constantly asking questions and arguing very effectively that the Corn Laws were creating poverty and distress. After one particular speech by Cobden, the Prime Minister, Sir Robert Peel, is said to have crumpled up his notes and said to a colleague: 'You must answer this, for I cannot'.

In 1845, the League changed its electoral tactics. As most of its support came from urban, industrial areas, Cobden now saw that the big challenge was to make inroads in the county seats, especially those that were largely rural but contained some urban areas. He realised that by buying property worth 40 shillings (£2) in county seats, the League could install its own supporters. In effect, it could buy votes in parliamentary elections.

The League was able to raise considerable sums of money from its wealthier supporters and now concentrated on buying enough votes in key constituencies to gain control of them. Several parliamentary seats were won in this way in 1845, but the League was still far from building up a large presence in the Commons. Furthermore, wheat prices were now lower than they had been for many years so that the League's speakers could no longer argue that the Corn Laws were keeping prices artificially high. At this stage, with the League's fortunes at a low ebb, the ending of the Corn Laws seemed a long way off. Yet a year later, in 1846, the Corn Laws were repealed. Before we can assess what impact the League had on the passing of repeal, we need to analyse why Sir Robert Peel, the Prime Minister, took the remarkable step of pushing through Parliament the bill that ended the Corn Laws.

Richard Cobden elected to Parliament: 1841

John Bright elected to Parliament: 1843

Key dates

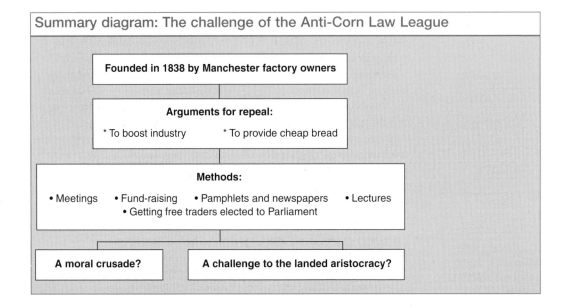

Summary diagram: The challenge of the Anti-Corn Law League

Founded in 1838 by Manchester factory owners

Arguments for repeal:
* To boost industry   * To provide cheap bread

Methods:
• Meetings   • Fund-raising   • Pamphlets and newspapers   • Lectures
• Getting free traders elected to Parliament

A moral crusade?

A challenge to the landed aristocracy?

2 | Sir Robert Peel and the Repeal of the Corn Laws

Key question
How do you explain the success of Peel's budgets?

When Peel came to power at the head of a Conservative government in 1841 he inherited a huge debt from the Whigs. Worse still, the country was slipping into economic depression. There had been a series of bad harvests after 1837, so bread prices were high, and exports had fallen. This economic crisis brought hunger, discontent, a revival of Chartism and the rise of the Anti-Corn Law League. Events seemed to be slipping out of the government's control. In this atmosphere, Peel introduced a dramatic budget in 1842. The key features were:

- the re-introduction of income tax
- the removal or reduction of tariffs on many imports.

Income tax

Key date
Income tax was re-introduced and many tariffs were cut: 1842.

In his budget speech in 1842, Peel painted a picture of a national emergency and then called for the re-introduction of income tax. It had only ever been raised before in war-time, but Peel convinced most of the Commons that now was the time for such a bold move. The tax would only be paid by those earning more than £150 a year, so that most of the working classes would be exempt. He argued that the poor already had to pay tax on their sugar, tea, soap, candles and many other articles of consumption. They could not take any more and their desperation was already evident in the upsurge of support for Chartism. Peel showed great political courage in asking the rich to pay more at this time of national distress. And it worked. The Commons agreed, responding to Peel's sense of urgency. Not only would this tax raise enough to clear the government debt, it would also enable Peel to reduce tariffs.

Reduction of import duties

Peel had been a member of the Liberal Tory government that had reduced tariffs in order to promote trade and industry in the 1820s (see pages 34–5). He now believed that tariff reduction was the key to economic recovery and social stability. He argued like this:

Key term
'To make this country a cheap country for living'
Peel said that this was his objective. His 1842 budget marked the first time that government economic policy had been used as a remedy for poverty and distress.

- if import duties on raw materials such as cotton and iron were reduced, it would stimulate those industries, leading to economic recovery
- economic recovery would mean more profits, more jobs, less distress and fewer Chartist disturbances
- if import duties on foodstuffs such as meat and potatoes were removed, it would help '**to make this country a cheap country for living**' which, said Peel, was one of his aims
- economic recovery and the relief of distress would take the sting out of Chartism, it would show that the ruling classes were willing to carry out reforms which would help the poor and thus help to restore social and political stability.

In the 1842 budget, the import duties on over 700 articles were either removed or reduced. Cheaper goods meant more were consumed so that, although tariffs were reduced on many items, the income generated by more imports meant that almost as much money was raised by government. The economic recovery began in 1843 and, by 1844, there was a surplus in government finances. Trade revived and unemployment fell. Support for Chartism declined, helped by better harvests, and the campaign of the Anti-Corn Law League lost some of its momentum. The budgets of 1842 and 1845 (in which even more duties were slashed) were an economic and political triumph for Peel.

Peel's decision

We cannot be certain when Peel became convinced that the Corn Laws would have to be repealed altogether. It might have been in the early 1840s. What we do know, and Peel knew, is that by 1845 Britain had moved a long way towards becoming a completely free trade nation. Peel's free trade policies were working: economic recovery was underway and there was less distress and disorder. The Corn Laws now stood out even more starkly as an economic oddity and were becoming harder to justify.

Key question
When and why did Peel decide to repeal the Corn Laws?

There were also longer-term issues that were pushing Peel towards complete repeal of the Corn Laws:

- Shortage of food: between 1815 and the 1840s, Britain's population had risen by nearly 50% and the food supply was barely able to keep up. Europe's supply of food was also overstretched under the strain of population growth. The opening of Britain's ports to foreign wheat might stimulate further continental production and lead to the opening of new sources of supply.
- The threat of the Anti-Corn Law League: the League had the potential to overthrow government by the landed classes. Peel knew that the Corn Laws – or the 'Bread Tax' as the League called them – were a powerful and hated symbol of the power of the landed aristocracy. Therefore repeal would remove what Peel feared most of all:

a war between the manufacturers, the hungry and the poor against the landowners [and] aristocracy, which can only end in the ruin of the latter.

With a general election due within a couple of years, Peel wanted to defuse the class struggle that Cobden and other League leaders were waging. Repeal would destroy this threat because the League would no longer have a reason to exist. It would also show the Chartists that a Parliament dominated by the landed classes was capable of passing laws in the interests of the nation as a whole. Above all, Peel wanted to carry out repeal when he and Parliament decided. The government did not want to be seen to be giving in to the League or the Chartists. In that way, the government's authority would be maintained.

Peel's biggest challenge was, first, to persuade his Cabinet and then Parliament. This would be particularly difficult as the majority of Tories were keen supporters of agricultural protection. As it happened, it was external events that forced the pace.

The Irish Famine 1845

On 26 August 1845, Peel received two letters.

Key question
What impact did the Irish Famine have on repeal?

- One was from Britain's representative in Prussia, the biggest of the German states. It said that if Britain kept the Corn Laws, Prussia would not sell any grain to Britain, even when the price of British-grown wheat was so high that imports were allowed. This was a serious threat to Britain's food supply.
- The second was from Ireland and told of the likely failure of the potato harvest. A mystery disease had already ruined the crop in mainland Europe. Now this 'potato blight' had reached Ireland and was likely to lead to starvation for millions of Irish, many of whom were completely dependent on the potato. Over the next five years, more than two million people either died of starvation or emigrated.

Peel now demanded an end to the Corn Laws to allow food from Europe to reach Ireland. He could have suspended the Corn Laws *temporarily* as this would have been much quicker and would have avoided splitting his party. But in fact, there *was* no source of additional food in Europe, and most of the Irish would be too poor to afford it anyway. It seems certain that Peel had already made up his mind to end the Corn Laws and that the Irish famine simply determined the timing of repeal.

Starving peasants at the gate of a workhouse in Ireland. There were, of course, no television pictures, but images like this appeared in newspapers and magazines so the effects of the famine could not be ignored in England.

Profile: Sir Robert Peel 1788–1850

1788	– Born in Tamworth, Staffordshire
1809	– Became MP for Irish pocket borough of Cashel
1812–18	– Chief Secretary for Ireland in Lord Liverpool's government
1817	– Became MP for Oxford University
1822–7	– Home Secretary in Liverpool's government
1828–30	– Home Secretary in Duke of Wellington's government
1829	– Steered Catholic Emancipation Bill through the House of Commons
1830	– Became MP for Tamworth on his father's death
1834–46	– Leader of the Tory/Conservative party
1834–5	– Prime Minister
1841–6	– Prime Minister
1846	– Passed Repeal of the Corn Laws and forced to resign
1850	– Died as a result of a riding accident

Peel's father had made a fortune as a cotton manufacturer in Lancashire. He then bought an estate at Tamworth in Staffordshire that brought with it a seat in Parliament, which he held until his death in 1830.

The young Robert Peel became an MP, for an Irish seat, at the age of 21. He became Chief Secretary for Ireland at the age of 24 and was in government for many of the remaining years of his life.

Like many of his generation who had grown up at the time of the French Revolution, he was committed to maintaining the monarchy and aristocracy. He feared the violence of a mob and believed that the government of Britain should be kept safely in the hands of the landed classes.

As Home Secretary, Peel was a Liberal Tory in his reform of the prisons and the penal system, making both of them more humane and efficient. He supported the privileged position of the Anglican Church in Ireland and had been a well-known opponent of Catholic Emancipation. So, when he steered the Bill for Catholic Emancipation through Parliament in 1829, he came to be regarded as a traitor by many Tories.

Peel opposed the Whig reform of Parliament, fearing that reform would 'open a door which I saw no prospect of being able to close'. However, he came to accept the Reform Act in his Tamworth Manifesto of 1834. He was Prime Minister for four months in 1834–5 and his government established the Ecclesiastical Commission to reform the Church of England. The Tories (re-branded as Conservatives from the mid-1830s) won the election of 1841 and Peel became Prime Minister again. His budgets of 1842 and 1845 contributed to economic recovery and won wide support, but his attempts to woo Catholic support in Ireland made him enemies in his party. His final act as Prime Minister was to push Repeal of the Corn Laws through Parliament. This split his party and led to his defeat and resignation. Nevertheless, his free trade policies earned him the praise of millions of Victorians, both at the time and in years to come.

Peel knew that the continuation of the Corn Laws would be seen as heartless while the Irish starved and rich landowners were protected. It would hand a propaganda gift to the Anti-Corn Law League and give a huge boost to their campaign outside Parliament. If Peel was to preserve a Britain governed by the landed classes, the Corn Laws would have to be repealed. The majority of the Tory party, however, saw things very differently.

The opposition to Repeal of the Corn Laws

The Conservative party believed that its members stood for two great principles: defence of the Church of England and of the landed interest. The party had fought and won the 1841 election on pledges to protect the Church and maintain the Corn Laws. And now Peel was overturning the second of these great principles – defence of the landed classes. To most Tories, the Corn Laws were not just tariffs protecting agriculture, but a symbol of aristocratic, landed rule and were part of what made Britain great. To these people, Peel was a traitor.

By December 1845 Peel had won over most of his Cabinet, but two members remained opposed to repeal. Peel knew that the Whigs were all in favour of ending the Corn Laws so he resigned, expecting the Whigs to form a government and carry through repeal. This would have the advantage of avoiding a split in the Tory party. However, the Whig leader, Lord Russell, was unable to form a government and Peel returned to power, now determined to push ahead.

The attacks which **Protectionist** Tories made on Peel in Parliament were savage. They tore into him in the debate on repeal knowing that there was considerable support in the countryside behind them. They were led by Benjamin Disraeli, who was to be a future Prime Minister. They knew that they could not stop repeal being passed because the Whigs, as well as the Cabinet and about a third of the Tory party, supported it, but they set out to destroy Peel.

The Bill was finally passed in June 1846, but, soon afterwards, 69 of the most bitter Tories joined with Whig, Radical and Irish MPs to defeat Peel's government on another issue. The Tories were to remain out of power for almost all of the next 30 years.

Peel's political career was ended and he died four years later after a riding accident. But to hundreds of thousands of working people he was a hero, their saviour, as the cartoon illustrates. He was portrayed as the man who had brought them cheap bread. Such was their gratitude, that 70,000 Chartists subscribed to a memorial to Peel in 1850.

Key question
Why was there such fierce resistance to repeal?

Key term

Protectionist
A supporter of economic policies to protect British farming from foreign competition.

Key dates

Repeal of the Corn Laws: June 1846

Death of Sir Robert Peel: 1850

This was the 'Monument to Peel' published in *Punch* magazine in 1850, the year of Peel's death.

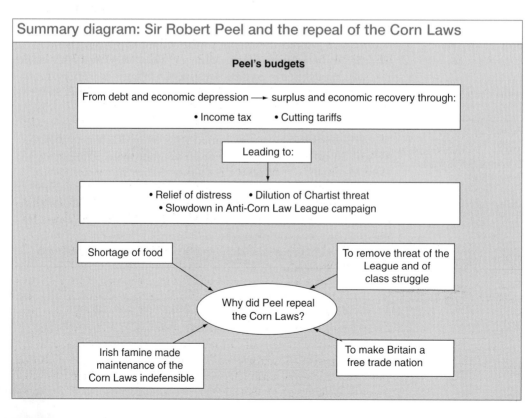

Summary diagram: Sir Robert Peel and the repeal of the Corn Laws

Peel's budgets

From debt and economic depression ⟶ surplus and economic recovery through:

• Income tax   • Cutting tariffs

Leading to:

• Relief of distress   • Dilution of Chartist threat
• Slowdown in Anti-Corn Law League campaign

Shortage of food

To remove threat of the League and of class struggle

Why did Peel repeal the Corn Laws?

Irish famine made maintenance of the Corn Laws indefensible

To make Britain a free trade nation

3 | Reform and mid-Victorian Stability

Key question
What was the impact of repeal?

Repeal of the Corn Laws did not lead to a huge influx of cheap wheat from abroad because there was no such source. The average price of wheat during the next 20 years was only a little less than the average before repeal. The difference was that, when the harvest was poor, imports (if available) prevented prices from rising too sharply. Nor did repeal ruin British farmers. In fact, they did very well in the 1850s and 1860s, responding to the growing demand for food from Britain's towns and cities.

The Anti-Corn Law League can take some of the credit for the repeal of the Corn Laws. They kept the issue at the forefront of politics and their arguments undoubtedly had an impact on the Whigs, as well as on Peel and some of the Tories. But, if the League aimed to dislodge the landed aristocracy from their position of predominance in British politics and society, they did not succeed. Throughout the nineteenth century, members of the landed classes continued to dominate Parliament and government. Most industrialists preferred to exercise their power and influence in local affairs.

The foundations of mid-Victorian stability

Key question
How important were Repeal of the Corn Laws and the 1832 Reform of parliament in laying the foundations of mid-Victorian stability?

The year 1848 was one of revolutionary upheaval in most European countries. Governments were overthrown and new political systems set up to replace them. Yet Britain's 'revolution' in 1848, the Chartist demonstration in London (see page 123), passed off peacefully and there was no change of government. Peel undoubtedly deserves some of the credit for this and for the years of **mid-Victorian** stability. Repeal of the Corn Laws, like Peel's earlier budgets, showed the working classes that that an aristocratic parliament could respond to their needs. The British State could be just and fair.

Key term

Mid-Victorian
The 1850s and 1860s are usually regarded as the mid-Victorian years. Queen Victoria was on the throne from 1837 to 1901.

Yet, perhaps, the Whigs deserve even more credit for the prosperity and stability of Britain in the 1850s and 1860s. The 1832 Reform Act, which had shocked Peel, won the middle classes over to the side of the aristocracy. The alliance between the landed and the industrial middle classes held firm in the crisis years of the late 1830s and the 1840s. Peel achieved much, especially in his budgets, but perhaps the Whigs achieved more. After all, they had had to fight for parliamentary reform and they provided most of the votes by which Repeal of the Corn Laws was passed.

Key date

Great Exhibition: 1851

The Reform Act and Repeal of the Corn Laws were just two of the reforms, albeit the most important ones, which enabled Britain to survive the stresses and strains it that faced in the years from 1815 to 1850. In 1851 Britain hosted 'The Great Exhibition of the Works of Industry of all Nations'. In fact, it was a showcase for *Britain's* achievements as the 'Workshop of the World', the world's leading industrial power. The exhibition also showed a nation at peace, as factories closed so that workers could travel by rail to see the exhibition. Britain had undergone reform, but not revolution, from 1815 to 1850.

The Crystal Palace was designed and built to house the Great Exhibition of 1851. It was erected in Hyde Park in London and made of iron and glass. After the exhibition was over it was taken down and rebuilt in south London. It burned down in 1936.

Study Guide: AS Question

In the style of OCR

To what extent was the Anti-Corn Law League responsible for the Repeal of the Corn Laws in 1846?

Exam tips

The cross-references are intended to take you straight to the material that will help you to answer the questions.

Re-read pages 131–7. In your introduction it would be a good idea to let the examiner know that you will be assessing the League's role in the context of other factors that contributed to repeal (e.g. Peel's policies, the Irish famine). In the main body of your essay, you should:

- explain, briefly, why the League was set up and what its methods were, and assess how important they were in the passing of repeal
- examine the significance of the League leaders, Cobden and Bright
- analyse Peel's role, e.g. how much his conversion to repeal was due to: (i) pressure exerted by the League, (ii) the path suggested by his earlier economic reforms (his budgets) and (iii) his political philosophy
- assess the effect of the Irish famine on Peel's decision to go for repeal in 1846
- judge how important was the role of the Whigs
- include any other factors you wish to consider.

Throughout the essay, you should:

- make judgements about the relative importance of different factors
- emphasise any links between them, e.g. between the effectiveness of League propaganda and Peel's decision-making.

In conclusion, you should highlight one or two key points about the League's role in repeal and weigh these up in relation to other factors. Lastly, you should arrive at the conclusion that is best supported by the evidence.

Glossary

Act of Union   The Act that ended Ireland's separate parliament and created the United Kingdom of Great Britain and Ireland.

Agricultural protection   The policy of protecting British farming from foreign competition.

Andover workhouse   In 1846, paupers in the Andover workhouse, who had been set the task of crushing animal bones for fertiliser, were so hungry that they had been found gnawing the bones in order to eat the marrow.

Anglicans   Members of the Church of England.

Aristocracy   Nobles, or peers, who inherited titles giving them the right to sit in the House of Lords.

'Bastilles'   Named after the Parisian prison, liberated in the French Revolution, which was seen as a symbol of oppression. Workhouses were often surrounded by high walls and were compared to prisons by their opponents.

Bill   A proposal for reform put forward in Parliament.

Birmingham Political Union   Formed in 1830 by Thomas Attwood, a banker from Birmingham, in order to campaign for Parliamentary reform. It attracted middle- and working-class support although Attwood did not believe in universal suffrage, but wanted the vote to be given to the middle classes who would then represent the views of the workers.

Canningites   Political allies and followers of George Canning. They were only a small group but they included two future Prime Ministers, Lord Melbourne and Lord Palmerston.

Capital offence   A crime carrying the death penalty.

Castlereagh   A government minister and leader of the House of Commons.

Catholic Emancipation   Allowing Roman Catholics the right to become MPs or to hold other public office.

Church of Ireland   Effectively the Irish branch of the Church of England.

Class legislation   A law passed to favour a particular class, in this case the landed class.

Cobbett, William   His *Political Register* was the most widely read radical journal in the years after 1815. To avoid arrest, he fled to the USA in 1817, returning in 1819. In 1832, he became the radical MP for Oldham, Lancashire.

Combination Acts   Laws passed to ban the formation of trade unions, or combinations, of working men.

Conservative   Came into use at the time of the Tamworth Manifesto when Peel promised that he would *conserve* the nation's institutions. Nevertheless, the term 'Tory' continued to be used as well.

Constituencies   Areas into which the country was divided up for elections. Most constituencies returned two MPs to Parliament.

Corn Laws   Tariffs, or import duties, on foreign wheat. In 1815, importing wheat was banned until British wheat reached 80 shillings (£4) a quarter (about 13 kg).

Deferential   Showing respect for people, in this case for those of a higher class.

Depression   A time when there is less demand for industrial or agricultural goods and so there are fewer jobs and more unemployment.

Dioceses   Areas into which the country was divided for church purposes. Each diocese had a bishop at its head.

Direct taxes   Taxes paid directly to the State, such as income tax.

Disenfranchising   Taking away the right to a seat in Parliament.

Ecclesiastical   Concerning the Church.

Evangelical Christians   Christians who believed that God called them to devote their time to good causes. They believed that better social conditions would give dignity to the poor and make them more responsive to religion.

Forty shilling freeholders   People who owned land or property worth 40 shillings (£2) a year.

Free trade   The idea that goods should be traded between countries without any duties (or tariffs) being imposed. Liberal Tory policies moved towards freer trade by reducing import duties.

French Revolution   A series of events, starting in 1789, which led to the fall of the monarchy and of the aristocracy in France.

Friendly Societies   Organisations to which members made a small weekly contribution and were provided with support in sickness or old age.

Fundholders   Those who had lent the government money during the French wars.

Guardians   Officials to be responsible for the administration of poor relief locally. In practice, many of the old overseers were elected as Guardians.

Habeas Corpus   The law that anyone arrested had to be charged with an offence and brought before a court. After the Latin for 'you have the body'.

Handloom weaver   A person who used a hand-powered weaving machine.

Hetherington, Henry   He led the 'war of the unstamped', the campaign against 'taxes on knowledge'.

Humanitarian   A person who works for the welfare of all human beings.

Humanitarianism   Working for the welfare of human beings, e.g. to reduce suffering. Instead of judging things by their usefulness, like the Utilitarians did, humanitarians were more concerned about the impact on human beings.

Import duties   Taxes (or tariffs) paid on imported goods.

Indirect taxes   Taxes paid as part of the price on purchases.

Irrigation   The supply of water to agricultural land.

Labouring poor   All those who earned their living by manual labour.

Laissez-faire   A French term, best translated as 'leave alone' or 'do not interfere'. The concept is associated with the free trade, economic ideas of Adam Smith.

Lichfield House Compact   Meeting of Whigs, Radicals and Irish MPs held at the house of Lord Lichfield in February 1835. They agreed to form an alliance to defeat Peel's Conservative government.

Lovett, William   One of the chief authors of the People's Charter. Like many other Chartists, he was imprisoned for a time. After his release in 1840, Lovett devoted his time to the improvement of working-class education and was much criticised by O'Connor for relying purely on 'moral force' Chartism.

Manhood suffrage   The right to vote for all adult men.

Middle classes   People below the landowning aristocracy, but who do not do manual labour. Many – manufacturers, merchants, bankers, shopkeepers – made their money from industry and trade. Others were members of the professions, such as lawyers, doctors, teachers.

Mid-Victorian   The 1850s and 1860s are usually regarded as the mid-Victorian years. Queen Victoria was on the throne from 1837 to 1901.

Municipal corporation   'Municipal' refers to local government. 'Corporation' means a town council.

National Charter Association   The NCA was a national, political organisation. It set up branches across Britain and members paid subscriptions to join. Many historians see it as the first independent, working-class political party, a forerunner of the Labour Party.

Nominee   Someone put forward for election. Over 200 MPs were nominated by an aristocratic patron who sat in the Lords. In other words, members of the House of Lords had huge control over the composition of the Commons. Often nominees were sons, younger brothers, cousins or friends of the family.

Nonconformists   Baptists, Quakers, Presbyterians and Methodists, etc.: Protestants, but not members of the Church of England.

Oastler, Richard   One of the leaders of the Ten Hours Movement. He opposed universal suffrage and trade unions, but believed that the rich and powerful had a duty to look after the poor and the weak. He opposed the new Poor Law and saw the workhouses as inhumane.

'Out of doors'   Used to describe political activity beyond Parliament, e.g. agitation 'out of doors' meant agitation in the country as a whole.

Overseers   The people appointed in the parish to collect the poor rate and decide how it was spent.

Parliamentary reform   Only a small number of people were allowed to vote for MPs. Parliamentary reform primarily meant granting this right to more people.

Paupers   Those who received benefits through the Poor Law system.

Penal code   A document, or series of documents, that states what penalties should be awarded for particular offences.

Picketing   Standing outside a factory or other workplace to discourage people from going to work.

Place, Francis   A tailor by trade who had been active in radical politics since the

1790s. He had been largely responsible for the repeal of the Combination Acts in 1824. Previously a supporter of manhood suffrage, Place now accepted the need to work with men of 'money and influence' in order to get the Reform Bill passed.

Pocket borough   A constituency that was in the control, hence the pocket, of a particular patron, usually a large landowner. The majority were controlled by Tories.

Political unions   Popular organisations created to campaign for reform of Parliament.

Polling station   A place for voting.

Poor relief   Support provided for the poor whether inside a workhouse ('indoor relief') or outside, in the form of money, food or clothing ('outdoor relief').

Prince Regent   Title given to Prince George when he acted as monarch during his father's illness.

Protectionist   A supporter of economic policies to protect British farming from foreign competition.

Radicals   Those who believed in the need for radical, or fundamental, reform.

Regent   The future king, George IV.

Repeal   Withdrawal (of laws, in this case).

Rotten borough   A borough with few or no constituents yet which returned at least one MP to Parliament.

Rough-sharpening   Sharpening swords in such a way that they would inflict 'a ragged wound', one more likely to fester and cause slow death.

Sacred Month   The proposal for a month-long strike if the National Petition was rejected.

Secret ballot   Casting a vote in secret, as is done today.

Seditious libel   Use of language encouraging rebellion against the State.

Smith, Adam   Scottish economist who argued that industry and trade flourished best when they were entirely free of government interference.

Speenhamland system   A method, devised in the Berkshire village of Speenhamland, for topping up farm labourers' wages, especially at a time of high bread prices.

Spinning jenny   A hand-driven machine which speeded up the process of spinning cotton into a thread that could then be used for weaving cloth.

Stephens, J.R.   A brilliant orator. He attacked the new Poor Law and became a fervent Chartist. He famously said, to a large crowd in Manchester, that universal suffrage was 'a knife and fork question'.

Swing riots   Rural riots in the south and east of England in 1830–1. The mythical leader of the riots was 'Captain Swing'.

Ten Hours Movement   A campaign started in 1830 for a 10-hour day for all workers. Support for the movement was organised through Short Time Committees, mostly made up of factory workers.

Tithe   A one-tenth tax of a person's income, payable to the Church.

'To make this country a cheap country for living'   Peel said that this was his objective. His 1842 budget marked the first time that government economic policy had been used as a remedy for poverty and distress.

Transportation   It was a common sentence for convicts to be sent to Australia for prison or compulsory labour.

Ultra Tories   Hardline Tories who resisted any constitutional change, especially the granting of political rights to Catholics.

Universal manhood suffrage   The right to vote for all men.

Universal suffrage   The vote for all people. In practice, at this time, it meant for all men, i.e. manhood suffrage.

Utilitarianism   A set of ideas developed by Jeremy Bentham who argued that government should be judged on its ability to promote 'the greatest happiness of the greatest number'.

Index